HD
62.5
.H46
1985

D0857530

Winners

THE SUCCESSFUL STRATEGIES ENTREPRENEURS USE TO BUILD NEW BUSINESSES

CARTER HENDERSON

HOLT, RINEHART AND WINSTON

NEW YORK

For my three Muses
Alexandra, Dorothy, and Vicky

Published by Holt, Rinehart and Winston,
383 Madison Avenue, New York, New York 10017.
Published simultaneously in Canada by Holt, Rinehart and
Winston of Canada, Limited.

Library of Congress Cataloging in Publication Data
Henderson, Carter F.
Winners: the successful strategies
entrepreneurs use to build new businesses.
Includes index.
1. New business enterprises—Management.
2. Success in business. 3. Small business—
Management. I. Title.
HD62.5.H46 1985   658.1'141   85–5511
ISBN: 0-03-001887-0

First Edition
Printed in the United States of America
10 9 8 7 6 5 4 3 2 1

Portions of Chapter 11, "What Do You Do After You've Won?"
have appeared in *Florida Trend*, March 1985

ISBN 0-03-001887-0

Acknowledgments

This book could not have been written without the help of more than 100 entrepreneurs who spent countless hours enduring my tape-recorded interviews, taking my follow-up phone calls, and answering my letters about the successful strategies they used to build their new businesses.

Well over fifty accountants, bankers, business school professors, tax consultants, venture capitalists, and others with expert knowledge of what it takes to be a winning entrepreneur also made valuable contributions to this book for which I am similarly grateful.

I am also indebted to my editor Jack Macrae III for judiciously pruning early drafts of the manuscript, to my production editor Shelly Perron for her invaluable insights, to the accounting firm of Deloitte Haskins & Sells for reviewing the manuscript as it neared completion, and to my literary agents Eric and Maureen Lasher for their unceasing encouragement to tell the story of America's entrepreneurs—the irrepressible ghosts in our free enterprise economic system.

Contents

Contents

1

The Greatest Game in Town

"We have lived through the age of big industry and the age of the giant corporation, but I believe that this is the age of the entrepreneur, the age of the individual. That's where American prosperity is coming from now, and that's where it's going to come from in the future."

—President Ronald Reagan
St. John's University
March 28, 1985

It happens every day of the week. Thousands of Americans summon up their courage and deal themselves into the greatest game in town—starting a business of their own.

Many fail. But a surprising number succeed—men and women of all ages, races, shapes, and sizes, who have become financially independent, self-fulfilled, and occasionally rich beyond their wildest dreams.

- Suzy Bass is a petite, divorced mother of two who has trouble seeing without her glasses, and knew practically nothing about business when she started up an emergency ice-delivery service in Austin, Texas, called Flash Cubes, whose sales are approaching $400,000 a year.
- Herb Colvin is a handsome black man who quit a good job, sold his car, and with his wife, Carole, launched Suncoast Supply, Inc., in Tampa, Florida, whose sales went from zero to $1,200,000 in two years and are still climbing.

- Chris Nguyen came to the United States from South Vietnam at age eighteen with no capital, little business experience, and a poor command of the English language, which did not stop him from opening an eggroll business in Omaha, Nebraska. He grossed $4 million in 1984.
- Ed Lowe was helping his dad haul sand and gravel when a neighbor asked him for something to put in the bottom of her cat box. Ed suggested absorbent clay granules, and Kitty Litter was born. Today the sales of Lowe's, Inc., in South Bend, Indiana, are running at $85 million a year, and Ed is off on new business adventures (with his company sending him $1 million a year for walking-around money).

These are a few of the winners you'll get to know in the pages of this book, along with entrepreneurial superstars such as Frederick Smith of Federal Express; Mary Kay Ash of Mary Kay Cosmetics; Bill McGowan of MCI Communications; John Hanson of Winnebago Industries; Xavier Roberts, who created the Cabbage Patch Kids; and the two Steves (Jobs and Wozniak) who started Apple Computer. You'll follow the business strategies that these and other winners used to make it in a business of their own.

You'll also meet nationally recognized experts who have helped countless winners prepare a business plan, raise start-up capital, develop new products, create effective advertising and public-relations campaigns, manage quality control, overcome crises, and eventually sell their businesses for a great deal of money.

And finally, you'll be initiated into the mysteries of everything from pricing your product, selling it by telephone, and reviving it when it gets tired, to keeping peace in a family-owned company, calculating how much your business is worth, and living the good life after you've worked your way to the top—if not before.

To most people, entrepreneurs are somewhat mysterious

figures whose names and faces seem to appear and disappear in the business pages of the local newspaper, or as "stars" in their own TV commercials. Many of them have built extremely profitable businesses, some amassing wealth the Astors, Rockefellers, and Vanderbilts might envy.

But what's their secret? How did they do it? And most important of all—can you do what they've done?

The Will to Win

Successful entrepreneurs have been studied in depth. No possibility has gone unexamined in the search to discover why they succeed when so many others fail. Sex, race, parents, age, capital, education, and more have been advanced as critical factors. But the most essential factor of all turns out to be the sheer will to win, or to "achieve" as Harvard psychologist David McClelland concluded in his landmark study *The Achieving Society*.

The late Ray Kroc, who built McDonald's into a multibillion-dollar fast-food empire, and his personal fortune to $500 million, put the will to win into a dictum borrowed from former President Calvin Coolidge, who is remembered to this day for his declaration that "the business of America is business." Kroc's advice:

> *Nothing in the world can take the*
> *place of persistence.*
> *Talent will not; nothing is more common*
> *than unsuccessful men with talent.*
> *Genius will not; unrewarded genius is*
> *almost a proverb.*
> *Education will not; the world is full*
> *of educated derelicts.*
> *Persistence and determination alone*
> *are omnipotent.*

The process of winning gets under way when you decide to start making things happen which will carry you forward to victory. Winning entrepreneur Nolan Bushnell, who co-founded the electronics game company Atari with five hundred dollars and sold it to Warner Communications four years later for $28 million, says it all comes down to one "critical ingredient, getting off your ass and doing something. It's as simple as that."

Ralph Lauren, the enormously successful fashion designer, followed Bushnell's "do something" advice when he stopped peddling neckties made by a Boston tie manufacturer and created a distinctive collection of his own to sell. "The world is not ready for Ralph Lauren," said the manufacturer. "But I felt it was," said Lauren. "I had talent. I wanted to go on my own. I *had* to go."

It's this boundless self-confidence, energy, and urge "to go" that starts most winners on their trek to prosperity. And at few times in U.S. history have the odds for grabbing capitalism's brass ring been more favorable than they are today.

Sweeping changes in almost every aspect of American life are opening up a dizzying number of new business opportunities for innovative entrepreneurs. The sharp increase in single parents and women in the paid labor force has created an unrelenting demand for more day-care centers and takeout restaurants. Breakthroughs in technology have spawned entire new industries, from bioengineering to video games and robotics. Government deregulation of the finance, transportation, and telecommunications industries has singlehandedly produced thousands of new businesses. And the nation's aging population is triggering a boom in nursing homes, retirement communities, and for-profit hospitals.

Would-be entrepreneurs have never had it so good. There are opportunities galore, and a dynamic free enterprise system to help turn their ideas into moneymaking ventures. In recent years, for example, there's been a quantum leap in the availability of venture capital, an explosion in the number of schools offering courses in entrepreneurship, the birth of specialized magazines such as *Inc., Venture, In Business,* and *Black Enterprise,* and the launching of more than sixty "incubators" where infant businesses can find affordable production space, support services, and advice, all under one roof. "Clearly," says Professor Karl H. Vesper of the University of Washington's School of Business Administration, "there's been a radical rise of entrepreneurship. "There's a latent lust for it in all of us— it's the American way."

The final report of the 1980 White House Conference on Small Business—which is scheduled to be repeated no later than September 30, 1986—summed it all up by noting that "small business is, in a deep sense, our birthright economy. It is through individual enterprise that we seize those rights of liberty and opportunity that we cherish—the freedom to take our lives into our own hands and pursue prosperity by our own lights; the chance to take risks on our own behalf. And the more people who assume risk and responsibility, the more citizens there will be with a direct stake in fortifying democratic government."

Eight Steps to Riches

So, if you want to get into business, and if you think you've got the determination to see it through, then you're ready to profit from the winning business strategies discussed in the pages of this book—strategies you can use to climb the following eight steps from an idea for a new product or service to a moneymaking business of your own (and the riches that await you when you reach the top):

1. Conceptualizing your new product or service.
2. Spotting trends in the economy that can stop your business idea dead in its tracks, or help power it to success.

3. Devising a credible business plan for developing and marketing your new product or service.
4. Assembling the resources needed to implement your business plan.
5. Launching your business.
6. Expanding your business.
7. Overcoming adversity and crises.
8. Breaking out into big-time sales and profits.

All new companies begin with a concept—an idea for something consumers want and will buy in sufficient quantity to build a flourishing business. It can be anything from Jim Henson's idea for a new kind of puppet he called Muppets (Kermit the Frog, Miss Piggy, and friends) to Ted Turner's decision to acquire a failing little UHF television station in Atlanta and turn it into "SuperStation" WTBS-TV, which uses the earth-orbiting satellite system to reach millions of cable-television viewers "across the country and beyond." "One good product or service," says E. Joseph Cossman, author of *How I Made $1,000,000 in Mail Order,* "can support you in style for the rest of your life."

Even the greatest idea for a new business, however, must be backed by a plan of action if it's to be transformed into a profitable company. Few venture capitalists will invest in your concept, or even condescend to talk to you about it, until they've reviewed your blueprint for making it happen. Thinking through such a strategy is doubly vital, since it forces you to focus on every step needed to get from concept to growing business.

The odds favoring any business plan's success can be increased if it's designed to either (1) hitch a free ride on one of the great trends rolling across the U.S. economy, or (2) avoid being crushed by their awesome power. The trend from an industrial to an information economy, as we know, is closing down steel mills in the Midwest while opening up bravura knowledge-intensive industries from Massachusetts' Route 128 to California's Silicon Valley.

Once you've completed your business plan, you must begin to assemble the resources needed to bring it to life. Although you, the entrepreneur, are unquestionably the spark plug required to start your new venture, the engine that will finally set it in motion is the free-enterprise system that is ready to supply your every need. Risk capital, skilled employees, production facilities, and eager suppliers are all poised to help you get a piece of the vast global marketplace, where well-conceived business ideas can produce mind-boggling results practically overnight.

Take the idea that came to two Montreal journalists, Scott Abbott and Chris Haney, in 1980, as they were sitting in the kitchen drinking beer and playing Scrabble for one hundred dollars a game. Out of the blue, Haney suggested they invent a game, and for reasons he can't remember, Abbott said it should be about trivia. So they cleared the kitchen table, roughed out the design of the game, and within one hour Trivial Pursuit was born. Abbott and Haney set up a company (along with Haney's brother and a lawyer), raised start-up money by selling nonvoting stock in the firm to thirty-two friends for two hundred dollars a share, and contracted with companies in Canada and the United States to assemble and distribute the game. "We had a near-maniacal belief that it would fly," said Abbott, and he was right.* In less than four years, Trivial Pursuit has racked up worldwide sales of $1 billion, going on $2 billion.

Starting a business before all the essential pieces are in place is dangerous, and can be very hazardous to your financial health. Federal Express is one of the most successful new businesses in recent memory. Yet investors refused to give

*James Dingwell, "Canada's Most Popular Export—Trivial Pursuit," *D & B Reports* (May/June 1984): 56–57.

founder Fred Smith the venture capital he needed to get his overnight small-package-delivery service off the ground until he produced an independent marketing study asserting that his concept was a potential winner. Smith produced not just one but two such studies, and got his money.

A new business can be launched from a backyard garage, as happened with Hewlett-Packard, Apple Computer, and numerous other winners, or it can occasionally emerge full-blown, as it did during Wall Street's highly speculative Go-Go Era during the 1960s when money manager Gerry Tsai's Manhattan Fund actually took in $247 million of its customers' money before it officially opened its doors for business. This is the trial-and-error stage, where strategic mistakes must be fixed in a hurry if the business is to survive and flourish. Arthur Jones, the ex-big-game-hunter and rattlesnake collector who founded Nautilus Sports/Medical Industries, puts it this way: "Success comes from good judgment. Good judgment comes from experience. Experience comes from bad judgment."

Pansy Ellen Essman, who started her business in a San Jose, California, chicken coop, learned this lesson when she began making and selling foam-rubber pillows to hold squirming infants while they were being bathed in the tub. Essman overpaid for materials because she didn't know how to bargain down prices. She had a trade-show booth palmed off on her that was located behind a door. She was forced to change the name of her product from Pamperette to Pansy-ette, and scrap $2,000 worth of packaging bearing the old name after receiving a threatening letter from Procter & Gamble (makers of Pampers). And as she started to succeed, competitors rushed in with knock-off products, forcing her to cut her prices. But Essman profited from her experience, and as a result her business grew tenfold in just four years, to $5 million, with gratifying profits.

Defying the Great Depression

Winning businesses can be launched under the worst possible conditions if the concept and business plan are right. This was proved over and over again during the Great Depression. The flamboyant Mike Cullen ("the world's greatest price wrecker") opened his King Kullen discount supermarkets on Long Island, and attracted shoppers from one hundred miles away. Charles Revson started Revlon on the road to a $2-billion company during the depth of the Depression, when he came up with the extraordinary concept that women would go wild over his nail polish if it was offered in a variety of colors with lipsticks to match. And on March 4, 1933, the very day a newly inaugurated Franklin Delano Roosevelt assured a worried nation that "the only thing we have to fear is fear itself," twenty-two-year-old Douglas Leigh started a new business that shortly began lighting up New York's Times Square with the most spectacular advertising signs the world had ever seen.

Once you've launched your business, it must grow or gradually die. Growth usually comes by selling more of your original product, and then expanding into related new businesses. This takes hard work and imagination of the kind that Lawrence "Herkie" Herkimer used to build a $20-million-a-year, family-owned business teaching kids to be cheerleaders. Herkie, who describes himself as the "oldest, fattest cheerleader in the business," started out as a member of the rah-rah squad at Southern Methodist University in Dallas from 1946 to 1948. Today he operates 350 cheerleading clinics attended by 150,000 youngsters a year, has launched special clinics for madcap humans who delight in climbing into a chicken suit and entertaining crowds at sporting events, and recently opened an office in Japan. Herkie began branching out into complementary businesses during the 1950s, and today his Cheerleader Supply Company controls 60 percent of the market for uniforms, pompons, and related paraphernalia made in his own factory or farmed out to other manufacturers.

As your new business climbs the learning curve, gains momentum, and begins profiting from the economies of scale, it's bound to encounter adversity and crisis. Building a company is "an experiment in terror and disorder," says Allen Michels, chairman of Convergent Technologies, Inc., of Santa Clara, California, and he is right. A hallmark of winning entrepreneurs, however, is their ability to overcome even the most seemingly insurmountable obstacles. Charles Lazarus unwittingly brought a crisis on himself when he sold his little Toys 'R' Us company to Interstate Stores, a poorly managed hodgepodge of retail outlets that went into bankruptcy eight years later, dragging Lazarus down with it. Lazarus kept building his business, however, and when Interstate finally emerged from bankruptcy, it did so as Toys 'R' Us, with Lazarus as chairman. Lazarus not only survived this debacle, but has since built the company into the nation's largest toy retailer, and his own net worth to more than $75 million.

If you can overcome the crises that sooner or later engulf all companies (even powerhouses like AT&T and General Motors are not immune), then you stand a chance of breaking out into the magic circle of roughly 15,000 companies with yearly sales of $25 million or more.

The challenge at this final stage of your company's growth is to maintain its entrepreneurial vigor. This can be done in innumerable ways:

- Introduce new products, as Fred Smith of Federal Express has done with ZapMail, an electronic transmission system that uses earth-orbiting satellites to guarantee delivery of documents and letters between communities in the United States within two hours.
- Acquire other companies. This helped make Los Angeles–based Pedus International the fastest-growing private com-

pany in the United States in 1984, according to *Inc.* magazine. "We're not building a business," says Pedus president Dick Dotts of his janitorial services company, "we're collecting entrepreneurs."

- Isolate your entrepreneurial high spirits from the debilitating bureaucracy that eventually infests every fast-growing business. You can do this by hiring a top professional manager to help run your company on a day-to-day basis, as the founders of Apple Computer, MCI, and Electronic Data Systems, among others, have done.

Business is the greatest game in town for most winning entrepreneurs who hang on for dear life, taking risks, feeling needed, making money, having fun, and controlling their own destiny until they can't make it into the office anymore. Arnold Bernhard, 84, who founded the Value Line Investment Survey during the Depression and is worth several hundred million, still lives in the Georgian Colonial house he bought in Westport, Connecticut, in 1944 for $55,000 and works in his midtown New York office with the aid of a wheelchair. And Rose Blumkin, who's in her nineties, continues to run the carpeting department of her sprawling store in Omaha's Nebraska Furniture Mart from a golf cart. "I come to work seven days a week," says Mrs. Blumkin, "and I never had a vacation in my life since I was six years old and helped my mother in a little store we had in Russia. I'll tell you something. People who are lazy don't last too long. The healthiest thing is to be with people. It occupies your mind, and you don't get senile. Why retire and wait for the devil? The devil will come anyway, and he'll come a lot sooner if you lay around and don't do nothing."

To the victors belong the spoils, and when you've finally made it in a business of your own, the world is your oyster—the private jets, yachts, opulent homes, professional football teams, and vineyards that are the rewards awaiting small- to medium-sized winners. If you're a really big winner, such as

TV Guide founder Walter Annenberg, and contribute generously to the campaigns of successful presidential aspirants, you could even find yourself in a top hat, a cutaway coat, and a royal, horsedrawn coach, clip-clopping through the streets of London on your way to Buckingham Palace to present your credentials to Queen Elizabeth II as the new United States ambassador to Great Britain.

All signs point to a resurgence of the free-enterprise spirit in this country, of men and women dreaming up innovative new businesses, assembling the resources needed to get them started, and then driving them forward to profitability.

Exactly how many entrepreneurs are launching new businesses in this country each year is a mystery. The most conservative estimate undoubtedly comes from Dun & Bradstreet, which tracks new business incorporations; it says these are running at a record rate of more than 600,000 a year, up from 100,000 or so in 1960. But U.S. Internal Revenue Service studies of the rising number of business tax returns filed from 1960 through 1982 show that only 16 percent were received from corporations—with the remainder coming from partnerships (8 percent) and sole proprietorships (76 percent). This suggests, and it is admittedly a guesstimate, that somewhere around four million new tax-filing businesses are being launched in this country each year (with a somewhat smaller number being closed down, bought up, or merged during this same period).

This may be true. The qualifier, however, is that the IRS considers anyone to be a sole proprietor who files a Schedule C (Profit or Loss from Business or Profession) with their 1040 form come April 15. All of these people certainly have the entrepreneurial spirit. But since most of them receive their primary incomes from wage-paying jobs, they are not true entrepreneurs in the Mary Kay Ash, Ted Turner sense of the word.

David Birch, founder and president of Cogentics, Inc., in Cambridge, Mass., which specializes in business data, believes about 1.2 million new businesses are being formed in the United States each year with a "huge never-never land of three million potential entrepreneurs out there who are doing something other than just working for somebody else."

But even this doesn't tell the whole story of the spirit of enterprise in America today. The rest of the story is hidden away in what Peter M. Gutmann, professor of economics and finance at the City University of New York's Baruch College, calls the "subterranean economy." Professor Gutmann estimates that "about a quarter of the U.S. labor force is engaged in underground activities," and that upwards of $420 billion worth of invisible, "off-the-books" transactions are thought to be conducted strictly in cash or barter every year. Investment adviser Doug Casey, author of *Crisis Investing,* predicts that the biggest growth industry between now and the year 2000 will be the underground "cash" tax-free economy, and that owning your own retail or small-service business will be the best way to profit from what he sees ahead. Entrepreneurs operating "off-the books" in the subterranean economy, needless to say, never end up in U.S. government statistical reports. What the government can't see, it can't count.

The Entrepreneurial Mystique

Nobody knows for sure what it takes to be a successful entrepreneur, but there are clues such as those found in a study done by Psychological Motivations, Inc., of Dobbs Ferry, New York, for Control Data Business Centers and *Venture* magazine. Psychological Motivations interviewed seventy-seven entrepreneurs whose businesses gave them personal incomes of $90,000 a year or more, and what they found was that quite a few of them:

- had quit their jobs to go into business for themselves because they felt victimized by their employers (the boss discriminated against women, inadequately rewarded moneymaking ideas, or simply didn't appreciate them enough);

- were offended by having to justify their ideas to superiors;
- did not fear failure, but used it as a source of motivation;
- were highly self-confident and fiercely competitive;
- viewed their businesses as playthings, so that work and pleasure blended together;
- were "excitement junkies" who thrived on risk and would start up new businesses once the old ones were successful but thrill-free;
- were open to new ideas of every kind;
- clung to rigid behavior patterns long after they needed to (e.g., they continued to grab a sandwich at their desks instead of lunching at clubs or restaurants);
- overwhelmingly named personnel as their number-one headache, even though the demands of running the business usually prevented them from paying much attention to their employees;
- were generally reluctant to seek outside help, partly because they got such a kick out of solving business problems themselves;
- were convinced that most people didn't know what the hell they were doing;
- believed their businesses were unique, and that no one else really understood them.

Perhaps the best-qualified person in the United States to distill the essence of winning entrepreneurs is John M. Albertine, president of the American Business Conference in Washington, D.C., whose members consist of the chief executive officers of one hundred companies with yearly revenues of from $25 million to $1 billion that have doubled their size in five years.

"These CEOs," says Albertine, "are free spirits with extraordinarily high intelligence, incredible energy levels, very creative, outspoken, opinionated, and totally tenacious. They are obsessed with success, and are eternally unsatisfied because their ego rewards come from great achievements made against great odds, and that's very fleeting. So they're continually searching for new ego-satisfying achievements, even though they're basically never going to be satiated. They also have patience quotients of zero. I'll give you an example.

"We have meetings all the time with leading politicians who like to be around winners. There's a mystique around winners. We once had a group of guys meet over breakfast with Ed Meese [Counselor to President Reagan and later named United States Attorney General]. Meese said, 'Look, I've had my breakfast, so why don't you get some eggs and I'll give you a little rundown on what've been up to in the Administration,' and he started to make a speech. He got about thirty seconds into it when Bob Dixon, chairman and CEO of Harvey Hubbel, Inc., said, 'You know, Mr. Meese, we've heard all this bullshit before, we don't want to hear it again, let's talk about policy, let's have a dialogue.' And Meese loved it. He's been back four or five times since."

Great entrepreneurs are clearly exceptional people with a maniacal will to win. "They are absolutely driven," says Benjamin Rosen, chairman of New York's Sevin Rosen Management Company, a venture capital firm with some $85 million invested in computers, electronics and other high-technology start-up companies, including two superstars—COMPAQ Computer and Lotus Development. "These people," says Rosen, "have total belief in their dreams, and are absolutely convinced they're going to succeed. They all have this desire to work twenty-four hours a day, seven days a week. They're willing to sacrifice their personal lives and make substantial financial sacrifices, all in the hope that it will pay off in the long run. And not just materially. They really believe something should be done and that they are the ones to do it."

"Be Stupid, Crazy, Naïve, and Lazy."

So if you think you've got this kind of straight-ahead drive and determination, if you're willing to make the sacrifices, take the risks, and work the hours, then chances are you too can make it in a business of your own—although you may be surprised at where you eventually end up.

At the dedication of the new five-building cinema-television center on the campus of the University of Southern California, an NBC reporter asked USC graduate George Lucas—who created the *Star Wars* trilogy—if his success had caught him by surprise. Lucas, whose gift of nearly $5.7 million had launched the center, replied that when he started out he was an "off-the-wall, avant-garde, underground filmmaker. I never thought in a million years that I'd be making theatrical features. It was a kind of a fluke. It's a strange life."

But if you're still convinced the entrepreneurial life is for you, then you can't do better than to follow the sage advice of super-entrepreneur Meshulam Riklis, chairman of the $2.4-billion Rapid American Corporation, whose counsel is "be stupid, be crazy, be naïve, and be lazy":

"Be stupid enough to think that what you want is attainable. Be crazy enough to give every bit of your energy to what you want to attain . . . crazy enough not to stop when people throw stones at you (a moving target is harder to hit!). Be naïve enough to understand that you can't take it all with you, so share with others as you go along. Be lazy enough to find someone else to do the work. You must have time to sit back and think."

Once you've decided to make the run, the next step is to decide what you're going to produce that consumers will buy in sufficient quantity and at a high enough price so you can make a nice profit, which, after all, is the name of the game.

2

It All Begins with a Concept

"You look at any giant corporation, and I mean the biggies, and they all started with a guy with an idea, doing it well."

—Irvine Robbins,
Co-founder,
Baskin-Robbins Ice Cream

"How many people do you know who've started an industry?" asks Ed Lowe of Cassopolis, Michigan, who looks like white-bearded country singer Kenny Rogers, and in 1947 stumbled on to the idea for Kitty Litter, which is today a $250-million-a-year business, of which Ed's privately owned Lowe's, Inc., controls some 34 percent, or $85 million.

The genesis of every new business is a concept: an idea for something you believe people want and will buy at a price that will pay you for the work needed to produce it. Concepts can arise out of anything, including helping the lady next door fill up her cat box.

When Lowe got discharged from the U.S. Navy after World War II, he joined his father, who was in the business of hauling sand, gravel, and concrete building blocks to construction sites, sawdust to meatpackers for smoking meats, and clay granules to factories for sopping up the oil and grease that messed up their floors.

Then one cold winter's night in 1947, Kaye Drapper, a neighbor, asked Lowe if he'd give her some sand for her cat box. Lowe gave her a bag of absorbent clay granules instead, and a week or two later she came back for more. "A couple of other people around town heard about it and wanted some," says Lowe, "and pretty soon folks around town were calling me 'the Cat Box King.' "

Lowe's next step was to buy some five-pound grocery bags, fill them with clay granules, and write on the side with grease pencil, "Kitty Litter. Takes the Place of Sand. Absorbs and Deodorizes. Ask Kitty, She Knows." Lowe threw the bags in the back of his truck, and took them along on a delivery he was making to South Bend, Indiana, where he stopped off at Davenport's Pet Shop. He told the owner what he had, and suggested that a five-pound bag might retail for sixty-nine cents. The owner said that was ridiculous, since he was already selling sand for cat boxes at a dime a bag. Lowe left him some Kitty Litter anyway, along with his phone number, and within days the man called, said he was selling the product for sixty-nine cents a bag, and wanted another delivery. Lowe bought some more bags, had some labels printed, and was in business.

Lowe began calling on pet shops with a bag of Kitty Litter under his arm and a shot glass in his pocket. He'd open the box, poke a hole in his mixture, pour a shot glass of water into the hole, and attempt to regale the startled pet shop owner with how well his product absorbed whatever a cat had in mind.

Then a cat show came to South Bend, and Lowe asked the president of the local cat club if he could have a booth to sell Kitty Litter in exchange for filling up the show's two hundred cat boxes with his product and keeping them spotlessly clean. The deal was struck, and Lowe says, "All the ladies loved Kitty Litter because it was the first cat show they'd ever been to that didn't smell."

Tidy Cat to the Rescue

By this time Lowe figured he had a potential winner on his hands, so he left his father's company, filled the back of his Chevy with bags of Kitty Litter, and started selling them to pet shops around the country for thirty-five cents a bag, which they resold for sixty-nine cents. Lowe had quantities of the product shipped to him in major cities such as Minneapolis and St. Paul, and once he had sold to a half-dozen pet shops or so, he'd sign up a wholesaler to handle the business while he went around trying to drum up more. Lowe charged wholesalers twenty-five cents for a five-pound bag of Kitty Litter, and shipped the product to them by the ton.

Over the next few years, Lowe traveled constantly. "I was out there where the rubber hits the road, working my whatchamacallit off," he says, "but it was worth it." Lowe blanketed the country with Kitty Litter, cornered 100 percent of the market, saw his sales hit several million dollars a year, started producing the clay granules used in Kitty Litter himself instead of buying them from others—and then he made a mistake. He sold one hundred pounds of Kitty Litter to a wholesale grocer for the usual twenty-five cents per five-pound bag. But the grocery wholesaler, accustomed to operating on smaller margins than pet shop wholesalers, resold it to his customers for thirty cents a bag, and they put it on their shelves priced at forty-nine cents a bag.

In no time, pet store owners were screaming at Lowe, which was very serious, since they were his major customers. "Cat products only got about three feet of space on grocery shelves in the mid-fifties," says Lowe, "so they weren't very important." Nevertheless, Lowe didn't want to lose this business, so he repackaged Kitty Litter under a new name—Tidy Cat—to be sold exclusively through grocery stores, while Kitty Litter itself was reserved for pet shops.

The only trouble was that the pet shop owners kept selling Kitty Litter for sixty-nine cents a bag, in competition with the forty-nine cents that supermarkets charged for Tidy Cat, and before long their sales started drying up. Lowe saw what was happening, and decided to begin selling Kitty Litter through supermarkets, with a value-added feature so they could charge more for it than they did for Tidy Cat.

Up to the mid-1950s, Lowe had no competition to speak of. Then a few "mom and pop" operators started entering the market with products like Cat Comfort, and as sales continued to grow, heavy hitters such as Hartz Mountain, Oil-Dri, and Clorox came in with their tremendous marketing clout. "The competition," said Lowe, "used delayed billing, they gave free merchandise, they gave free distribution, they made pie-in-the-sky promises on advertising which in many cases never came through, but that didn't bother us. We did our fair share of advertising, we always hired the good guys, we treated our customers right, we had a quality product, we gave service, and never underestimated the value of the names Kitty Litter and Tidy Cat."

This strategy has paid off for Lowe and his company, which is still the nation's leading maker of cat-box fillers and related products, with a fast-growing business overseas. Tidy Cat is the largest-selling cat-box filler in the United States, and Kitty Litter is the number-one premium-priced brand. Lowe's, Inc., with its five manufacturing plants and sixty warehouses, also produces cat-box fillers for many private-label customers throughout the country, and has started introducing new product lines that use absorbent clay granules for other purposes. One of these, called Safety Absorbent, is used to dry up oil, grease, water, and other spills common in manufacturing plants, while Corz-O-Nite handles heavy-duty spills endangering the environment.

Ed Lowe's thirty-five-year-old Kitty Litter company is now

running itself and he is looking for new worlds to conquer. "I'm not a manager," says Lowe, "I'm a builder. I like to get in on the ground level, to start something up. Most of the fun is in the planning. Then I like to leave the management to somebody else." Lowe takes $1 million out of his Kitty Litter business each year, and is currently investing most of his time in a new company called Lowe's International, Ltd., which is committed to world trade.

On a recent Saturday, I found Ed busily designing a bag for a new kind of cat-box filler he's all excited about, along with two new products he's importing from overseas. One is a baseball cap that plays "Take Me Out to the Ball Game" when you put it on your head, and the other is an easily adjustable wrench that he thinks has great promise. "I've just had three million of these things made in the People's Republic of China," he says. "God Almighty, I sure do hope they sell."

The $2-Billion Kid

Most business concepts are copies of already successful enterprises: another bakery, flower shop, or bowling alley. There's nothing wrong with following in other winners' footsteps, especially if you can put an imaginative new twist on their concepts. For example, entrepreneurs have been making dolls for centuries. But only once in a blue moon will you get a runaway best-seller like Raggedy Ann, Barbie, and now the Cabbage Patch Kids.

The pudgy-faced Cabbage Patch Kids are the brainchild of junior-college dropout Xavier Roberts, a stubby, bearded man perennially dressed in open-necked shirt, blue jeans, snakeskin boots, and cowboy hat, who began selling his "soft sculpture" dolls—no two of which were alike—in and around his hometown of Cleveland, Georgia, when he was barely twenty, and working fulltime at the nearby Unicoi State Park's gift shop.

Today, recently dirt-poor Xavier Roberts is one of the richest young men on earth, and he owes it all not to his dolls' good looks (they are downright homely), or to their low price (well over 100,000 early versions were sold at $125 or more apiece), but to an inspired concept that he stumbled on while exhibiting his dolls at country fairs and craft shows. Roberts would set up a booth, arrange his dolls in lifelike settings, and, to get a conversation going with passersby, would pick one up and say, "She's red-haired and short-tempered," or "She doesn't like cookies," and almost before he knew it, he'd made a sale. A little later, some buyers would send Roberts letters about how their "baby" was doing, which gave him his fabulous concept.

Roberts decided his creations were not dolls at all, but "Little People" born in a cabbage patch. He gave each of his kids a name and a birth certificate, and insisted that "prospective parents" take an "Oath of Adoption," which reads, "I solemnly promise to be an understanding parent to my best ability, to provide for his/her needs, handle with care, love and nurture with most of my affections, train him/her up in the way he/she should go, and cherish my role as an adoptive parent of the only Cabbage Patch Kid of his/her kind in the world."

Many of Roberts's Little People are born in the Babyland General Hospital, an old clinic in Cleveland, Georgia, which Roberts turned into an emporium where salespeople are dressed like doctors and nurses, and where "prospective parents" can see their new babies lifted out of the cabbage patch and then slapped on the rump by a "doctor" wearing a white coat (with stethoscope around his neck and surgical mask over his nose). As the "prospective parents" head for the Adoption Room to take the Oath (and settle up with the cashier), they will likely pass by Babyland General's Operating Room, its Nursery, where newborn infants can be observed through a plate-glass window, and a schoolroom where kids can be seen busily at work doing their numbers and learning their ABCs.*

The buying public has obviously been turned on by Roberts's fantasy, as total sales of his Little People and licensed Cabbage Patch merchandise are currently zooming toward the $2-billion mark.

An ideal way to start a copycat business is to find one you like and get the owners to tell you how they do it (they will most likely talk your head off—particularly if they live in another town where they won't risk having you as a competitor).

The next step is to try to bring a fresh conceptual insight to your copycatting, which can pay off handsomely. Take something as simple as making it easier for consumers to buy or use everyday products, an idea that has given birth to vast new industries while animating the English language with adjectives such as *fast-food, takeout, drive-thru,* and *throwaway,* and nouns like *credit card, convenience store,* and *doggie bag.*

House-Call Bodybuilding

In Beverly Hills, California, Hans Buhringer has introduced a health club he delivers to his clients' front doors. Each weekday at 6:00 A.M., seventeen-foot-long black trucks loaded with $10,000 worth of rowing machines, electric muscle stimulators, biofeedback devices, and vitamins pull up to the homes of actors, agents, and rock stars who pay forty-five dollars for a half-hour workout. Buhringer says he's now franchising his mobile "Now or Never" health clubs, and is in the process of introducing a line of vitamin/mineral supplements, workout equipment, and clothes.

*A rollicking description of Xavier Roberts's career can be found in William Hoffman's colorfully illustrated *FANTASY: The Incredible Cabbage Patch Phenomenon* (Dallas: Taylor Publishing Co., 1984).

If added convenience is the leading technique for transforming familiar products into new businesses, then the runner-up is price—figuring out how to fill consumers' needs for less money, which usually means providing less service.

Price-cutting stockbrokers such as Charles Schwab & Co. and the Quick & Reilly Group, Inc., for example, are able to charge customers a much smaller commission for buying or selling shares of stock for them, because they don't offer investment research or advice, as do Merrill Lynch and other big-name brokers. An estimated 120 discount brokers have sprung up since 1975, when Congress gave the green light to unfixed prices, and according to Quick & Reilly co-founder Leslie Quick, Jr., they are doing very well indeed.

"In 1975," says Quick, "discount brokerage accounted for less than one percent of retail stock trading, in 1984 it was running at between 15 percent and 16 percent, and in 1985 I can see it increasing to 20 percent. And keep in mind that the total stock-trading pie we're getting a piece of is also increasing. In 1983, daily trading volume on the New York Stock Exchange totaled 85.3 million shares, but sometime in 1986 I can see that figure hitting 150 million shares."

One indication of the price-cutters' success is the way they're being snapped up by cash-rich buyers. Charles Schwab & Co., the nation's biggest discounter, was bought by BankAmerica Corporation for $53 million, while the Chicago-based Rose & Co. was grabbed by the Chase Manhattan Bank.

Variations on this concept are popping up all over the place, and more are bound to appear as the deficit-ridden U.S. economy continues to weaken and consumers grow more cost-conscious. Discount dentists, budget motels, off-price clothing stores, walk-in medical emergency rooms, no-frills airlines, you-haul movers, and plain-pine-box undertakers are all examples of businesses created by the simple expedient of eliminating services and cutting prices.

On a par with "off-price" is "do-it-yourself," which allows

thrifty consumers to save money while learning valuable and mind-expanding new skills. The assemble-it-yourself kit business, for example, is prospering by selling consumers everything they need to make their own high-quality stereos, backpacker vests, suitcases, color TVs, personal computers, and even automobiles at substantial savings. The gardening industry is supplying tools, fertilizer, bug killers, and kindred products valued at $13 billion annually to some 34 million families producing homegrown food for their tables.* And the do-it-yourself home-improvement business, which grew sixfold from $6.4 billion in 1970 to an estimated $38.6 billion in 1984, is projecting sales of $75.4 billion a year by 1990.† A variation on the home-improvement concept is do-it-yourself homebuilding, which is providing rewarding life-styles to a canny group of entrepreneurs, including Pat and Patsy Hennin in Bath, Maine.

Do-It-Yourself Educators

"We've been profitable since day one," say the Hennins, who own the eleven-year-old Shelter Institute, which teaches people how to design and build their own homes for a fraction of what an architect and general contractor would charge. The Institute's steady growth to twenty-one employees and an annual enrollment of 1,500 students has made it Bath's second largest business after the Bath Iron Works, which turns out cargo vessels and warships.

The Hennins decided to launch the Shelter Institute after building their own passive solar house for $5,000 and in the process becoming convinced that housing-construction techniques had evolved over the years for the ease of the builder

---

*Gardens for All, "1984–85 National Gardening Survey" (Burlington, Vermont, 1984):1–2.
†Do-It-Yourself Research Institute, *The DYI Consumer Market: 1984 Reference Guide* (Indianapolis, 1984): 99.

rather than for the good of the owner. So they decided to try to teach homebuilding as a rational process. They were certain that if people had the right information, they could do a better job of designing and building their own houses to fit their sites, climates, pocketbooks, personalities, and even fantasies.

On the day I visited the Shelter Institute, some 160 new students were trooping up to the second floor of the old Masonic Hall, which the Hennins have converted into a complex of classrooms and shops selling books, architectural and building supplies, and a line of hand and power tools.

Pat begins the three-week course with a four-hour lecture in which, among other things, he tells the students, "There's nothing in building a house you can't do for yourself. You can usually build a house for the $10,000 to $25,000 the bank demands as a down payment, and four years later you can sell it for $100,000. Nowhere else can you make such an assured profit, and nowhere else can you use your hands and mind together to produce something so worthwhile while having so much fun."

Once Pat finishes his lecture and Patsy has shown a twenty-four-minute color film about the Institute, called "A Place to Live," the students begin standing up and introducing themselves. There's a computer programmer from San Antonio, a librarian from Wisconsin, a New York City Police Department detective, a marine biologist from Florida, an employee of the U.S. Department of Energy in Washington, D.C., a Navy helicopter pilot, a "retired mother," and an Alaskan fisherman who's just bought forty acres of land and wants to build a log cabin.

By tomorrow morning, these students—from teenagers to white-haired oldsters—will be caught up in a hectic round of class lectures, skills workshops, slide presentations, films, parties, bull sessions, and visits to some of the houses built or under construction by Shelter Institute graduates living near Bath.

In their three weeks at the Institute, the students will be exposed to every aspect of homebuilding, from selecting a site to buying homeowners' insurance. They'll learn about the properties of wood and other construction materials, about sheathing, fastenings, insulation, roofing, wiring, plumbing, heating, and chimney building. They'll also learn about more than a dozen different kinds of foundations, fifteen types of framing, and the many ways to build a house so it uses a minimum of energy for heating and cooling. In Maine, where bone-chilling winter comes early and stays late, and where some homeowners' heating bills exceed $5,000 a year, conserving energy is a high-priority item.

Toward the end of the course, Shelter Institute students design and make a scale model of the house they want to build when they get back home. If construction questions arise after they leave Bath, they can call Pat on a special number any morning from 7:00 to 8:00 A.M. and get the answer. If they're still in a quandary, they can return to the Institute for a weekend and have its teachers (many of whom were once lawyers, economists, builders, engineers, and doctors) tear their plans and models apart and reassemble them so they'll work.

The Shelter Institute's product is education, which Pat says is an extremely personal business. "Patsy and I are here slugging it out all the time. We also work hard to make our teachers feel that everything they do here is terribly important, and this rubs off on the students. We force our teachers to train, and we all huddle in a room together for ten days straight, four times a year, just grinding through all this stuff. It takes more than credentials to teach here, and there's no such thing as tenure. The minute a teacher starts to slough off, he's out."

Pat and Patsy Hennin believe that owner-built houses are the wave of the future. "We hear," says Patsy, "that 20 percent of the new houses in this country are being built all or in part by their owners." This would seem to be part of the self-help boom taking place throughout the United States these days in health care, auto repair, leisure (studies indicate that one out of ten Americans is a jogger), and even book publishing. "We're certainly experiencing this trend at the Shelter Institute," says Pat Hennin, "as more and more people keep coming here whether times are good or bad. It doesn't seem to make any difference."

The Shelter Institute is capitalizing on this momentum by adding new courses such as Post-and-Beam Construction, and by moving into new businesses. The Hennins now sell videotapes describing how to design and build your own home, they've developed a "Build Your Own" boardgame that takes up to six players through every step of the homebuilding process, and they've become dealers for an extensive line of solar energy and conservation products for use in the home.

But the Hennins' most surprising strategic move is a foray into the aviation business. They are now authorized dealers for the Lazair Ultralight airplane (an ultralight is defined by the Federal Aviation Administration as a single occupant plane that weighs under 254 pounds, has a top speed of 64 miles per hour, and is able to fly as slowly as 23 miles per hour.) The Hennins sell build-it-yourself Lazair Ultralight kits for $5,400, and offer construction space and free supervision during the 150 to 200 hours it takes to assemble the airplane. A certified flight instructor is also on hand, and after five to ten hours of lessons, the Hennins say, "You'll be able to take your Lazair up with the birds."

There are countless other strategies for giving old concepts a new lease on life. Miami's Key Pharmaceuticals has turned itself into one of the fastest-growing companies in the booming health-care industry by finding new ways to administer drugs. One of Key's blockbuster products is an adhesive patch that can be stuck on a patient's chest, where it will deliver controlled amounts of familiar medications over many hours. The seasoned concept behind the Lawn Doctor has been appropriated by the Computer Doctor, a nationally franchised chain specializing in at-home and bring-in computer maintenance. And John Margaritis has upgraded his check-cashing service, known as the California Currency Exchange, by adding a fleet of vans that allow Angelenos to cash their weekly paychecks in their employers' parking lots.

"Believe It or Not" Zippers

At first glance, something may look like the best of all possible foundations on which to build a new business. But you never know. One negative factor is the always-present suspicion that surrounds any new product, a hazard that nearly deep-sixed the ingenious Talon zipper, patented in 1883.

Talon's zipper looked like a winner if there ever was one. No more ugly buttons messing up clothes, no more need to painstakingly sew buttonholes, no more fumbling around, trying to get a dozen buttons into a dozen holes in order to walk down the street with dignity. Yet according to early salesmen's reports, prospects weren't interested in Talon's zippers ("Can't see increase in cost of garments . . . too much trouble to take up with pants makers . . . shop people want more money for applying it . . ." etc.).

Talon had every right to be discouraged, but instead it began pushing zippers for use in products other than clothing. This tactic broke the market wide open. Zippers were soon being used in money belts, tobacco pouches, purses, vacuum cleaner bags, overshoes, and the like. By the 1930s, sales were roaring along at such a clip that Talon had to keep hiring workers at its plant in Meadville, Pennsylvania—a fact that Robert Ripley saluted in his "Believe It or Not" comic strip under the headline THE TOWN THAT NEVER KNEW THERE WAS A DEPRESSION.*

Thomas Edison encountered an even more serious problem

---

*Sidney Furst and Milton Sherman, eds., *Business Decisions That Changed Our Lives* (New York: Random House, 1964), 115–133.

following his invention of the electric light, which attracted luminaries such as Wall Street tycoon J. P. Morgan, actress Sarah Bernhardt, and the President of Mexico to his house at 65 Fifth Avenue in New York City, to see this magical new form of illumination.

The trouble was that there was no infrastructure to power Edison's electric light. So to make a commercial success out of his invention, Edison had to build the electric utility industry. He had to create electricity generating and distribution equipment, a manufacturing company to make it, an engineering organization to install and maintain it, and a network of central power stations to produce and distribute the resulting power. Edison, towering entrepreneur that he was, did this, and within twenty years electric utilities were in operation throughout the United States.*

The lesson to be learned from both Talon's zipper and Edison's electric light, of course, is that it's a lot easier to get your new product into the hands of consumers if the system to manufacture and market it is already in place.

Concepts for moneymaking new products can arise out of almost any human experience, as is demonstrated by the case of Norman Gardner, who heads his own public-relations firm in Montreal. Gardner wanted to invent a new kind of paper that couldn't be photocopied. So he gave his secretary one hundred dollars and told her to go to a drugstore and load up on hair creams, nail-polish remover, and whatever else she could find to be rubbed on sheets of paper to see if they'd prevent them from being copied.

Nothing worked, until Gardner accidentally spilled coffee on some paper. This did the trick, producing totally black copies. Gardner set up NOCOPI ("no copy") Paper, Inc., hired a McGill University chemist to find the magic ingredient in cof-

*Robert Conot, *A Streak of Luck* (New York: Seaview, 1979) 118–192.

fee, and signed agreements with a Swiss firm to produce his product, and the Boise Cascade paper company to sell it to a market that, according to one estimate, could be worth $400 million a year in the United States alone.*

One of the richest hunting grounds for new concepts is big business itself, where employees are constantly making their fortunes from concepts that top management has missed, ignored, or rejected.

Harvard Business School graduate Ruth Owades was the marketing director of a mail-order company when she suggested that it court wealthy gardeners with a new catalog filled with fancy tools, ornate planters, attractive lawn furniture, and other upscale goodies. Owades's market studies indicated that her catalog was a winner, and when her bosses said "nothing doing," she incorporated the concept as Gardener's Eden. Four years later Owades sold her company for close to $1 million.

The trick, in many cases, is to think up ways to add new value to a product or business that already exists. One way to do this is by analyzing how the product or business actually works, and then figuring out how additional value could be created if things were done differently.

Dr. Alan Zakon, who heads the Boston Consulting Group, illustrates this technique with term insurance. Zakon believes term insurance was born when somebody realized that a regular insurance policy consisted of savings and protection, and that if you removed the savings part you'd have a new product—term insurance—for those who just wanted to buy protection.

This is a simple case of "unbundling," which street-smart entrepreneurs use all the time to create new value. Jimmy Ling used it back in 1967 when he was chairman of Dallas's LTV Corporation and bought Wilson & Company, a meat-

*Jim Ostroff, "Paper That Can't Be Copied," *Venture* (April 1984): 127.

packing company with interests in sporting goods and pharmaceuticals. Ling promptly "redeployed" Wilson's assets into three new corporations, offering minority interests in them to the investing public.

Investors weren't too excited about buying into Wilson & Company, which continued in the meat-packing business. But they immediately snapped up shares of Wilson Sporting Goods, serving the lush leisure market, and Wilson Pharmaceutical & Chemical, supplying the fast-track health-care industry. Ling had shown Wall Street that Wilson's parts were worth more individually than together, prompting Wilson & Company president Roy Edwards to call him "the Galileo of American enterprise."*

The Devil and King Saud

The ultimate concept is a "niche" business—a kind of proprietary island where there are eager customers and few if any competitors. Over the years, this dream has come true for thousands of imaginative entrepreneurs, and today it's coming true for thousands more, thanks to opportunities arising from changes in technology, demographics, government deregulation, world trade, and American life-styles. The only limit on unearthing a profitable "niche market" is your own imagination, which, as Albert Einstein once remarked, "is more important than knowledge."

The beauty of imagination is its ability to cut through to the heart of the matter. This is charmingly illustrated by Robert Lacey in his book *The Kingdom: Arabia & The House of Saud*, in which he tells the story of a great holy man who believed the radio stations being built throughout Saudi Arabia by the

---

*Stanley H. Brown, *Ling: The Rise, Fall, and Return of a Texas Titan* (New York: Bantam Books, 1973), 19, 137–138.

country's founder, Abdul-Aziz ibn-Saud, were the work of the devil. The devil obviously carried the radio programs through the air himself, and the holy man insisted that the satanic stations be closed down. King Saud would have been hard-pressed to ignore this request, had he not hit upon an imaginative way to convince the holy man that the devil was not involved.

"Would Satan carry God's word?" King Saud asked the holy man. "Verily, O Long of Life," the holy man replied, "you joke with me. For you know, and I know, that Satan would not carry God's word one inch." Whereupon King Saud had the Imam of the Great Mosque in Riyadh go to the radio station there and read some verses from the Koran. As soon as the holy man heard the sacred words crackling through the air, he blessed the radio as God's own miracle, as did all the other holy men in the Kingdom.

In a dazzling leap of imagination, New York playwright David Landau, 29, found his niche producing "participatory murder mysteries" at upwards of $3,000 apiece for private parties and corporate clients such as General Foods and Seagram's. Landau's Murder to Go, Inc., will sprinkle actors among the guests at your party, including a "murderer" and a "victim." Only you will know who the killer is until a "police inspector" arrives to grill your guests and unmask the perpetrator.

Technology produces more niches than anything else, although, as Hertz, MCI, Federal Express, and others will attest, they don't last long before competitors come rushing in—frequently turning a niche into a major new market benefiting everyone, including the company that got there first. It's been said that the best thing that ever happened to Hertz was Avis, whose advertising helped sell millions of people on the novel idea of renting an automobile.

A very big payday awaits you, of course, if you have the

imagination to track down a mini-niche within an explosively growing maxi-niche.

The Katzes Find Their Niche

Harriette Rose and her husband, Dr. Martin Katz, a cardiologist, uncovered a mini-niche in the giant U.S. food-service industry, which they've since turned into a marvelous little business.

As it happens, one of the fastest-growing maxi-niches in the food-service industry is the catering business, in which some 3,300 firms compete for a market valued at close to $1 billion a year. The Katzes figured that well-heeled people interested in buying a catered party wouldn't have the time or know-how to choose the best vendors, so they set up New York's Gourmet Advisory Services, Inc., to do it for them.

The Katzes call themselves "party planners," and for a 15-percent commission they'll arrange the menu, the decor, even the mood (low lights, ashtrays in place) for a catered affair such as a real-estate developer's all-desserts Christmas buffet, held in Manhattan's posh Helmsley Palace Hotel. Mrs. Katz, radiant in a gold lamé gown, presided over the party, making certain that the three thousand individual desserts and glazed fruits—including four hundred assorted chocolate truffles and Moroccan crepes freshly prepared before the guests—were served without incident.

Once you've colonized a profitable niche, you can make even more money expanding it.

Todd Axelrod found his niche in selling attractively framed historical documents to customers who hadn't previously even thought about acquiring a letter signed by George Washington, or a copy of the Thirteenth Amendment to the United States Constitution signed by President Lincoln and the Civil War Congress. Axelrod opened his first American Museum of Historical Documents retail gallery in a luxury Las Vegas shopping mall in 1982, has since opened another one in Dallas, and plans to open an additional eight to ten over the next four years in various parts of the country.

David Landau expanded his Murder to Go niche by producing mock homicides for resort hotels and cruise ships, co-producing a mystery film called the "Jokers Wild," and creating a "Murder to Go" home party game for Ideal/CBS Toys, Inc.

Among the dangers of playing the niche business game is that it might not work out, or you may stay mired in a failed niche longer than you should. This happened to New York City's First Women's Bank, which was founded in 1975 and, in addition to fairly severe top management problems, has not been able to make it by concentrating on female depositors and borrowers. In 1984, First Women's Bank hired Jill M. Considine as its new president and chief executive officer after going without one for seven months. Considine, who ran Bankers Trust's $20-billion commercial-loan portfolio before joining First Women's Bank, believes she's helped this tiny institution, which has just thirty employees and $40 million in assets, find its niche before she resigned to serve as New York's state superintendent of banks.

"The niche we discovered—and I hate to say it, but it really discovered us—is the small-business owner in New York City," says Considine. "New York is filled with small businesses, even though it's thought of as the home of Exxon and other giant corporations. New York, in terms of banking, is really made up of mega-financial institutions, and the small-business person tends to fall through the cracks. The cost structure of a large bank may preclude it from making a loan smaller than $1 million. What's more, an Exxon probably knows many years in advance what its borrowing requirements are going to be, and large banks like Chase or Bankers Trust also know where they're going far in advance.

"But small companies—the fastest-growing number of which are run by women entrepreneurs—are a lot more flexible.

They're reacting to opportunities all the time. And when they come into a large bank, they do not want to deal with the most junior person there. They want to meet with the senior credit officer or the president, and that's what First Women's Bank can provide. The bank has also gone a step further," Considine adds, "and is looking for a niche within this niche. The one it's currently thinking of targeting is small service businesses."

Don't fret, by the way, if you can't think up a winning concept. There are other ways to approach this problem, and among the best is to simply ask people what they need that's not already available in the marketplace, and then make it.

Terry Tanner did that more than twenty years ago, when he was a thirty-six-year-old physician in St. Petersburg, Florida, who wanted to build his own business but had no idea what to make. So he invited some doctor and dentist friends in for a brainstorming session. Tanner's first moneymaking idea came from one of the dentists, who said he was constantly running out of batteries for the flashlight he used to peer into his patients' mouths. Said he, "Why don't you make a flashlight I can throw away when its batteries are dead?"

Tanner liked the idea so much that he asked his only employee at the time—an engineer he had hired away from Honeywell—to design a disposable flashlight, which shortly thereafter was being snapped up not only by dentists and doctors across the country, but by corporations like Xerox and IBM. This concept has since been followed by others that have transformed Tanner's company into a medical-products conglomerate with sales of $21 million in 1984 (after spinning off its consumer-products division to Fuqua Industries for $5 million). The name of Tanner's company? Concept, Inc.

Two ex-employees of IBM named Timothy P. Ahlstrom and F. Morgan Lamarche decided to launch a new computer company in 1978, even though they didn't have a clue as to what to make. So they invited a few data-processing managers in for a day-long gripe session, hoping to stumble on a concept nobody had thought of in this industry crawling with some of the fastest minds on earth.

One complaint that kept reappearing was the difficulty that the data-processing managers were having in anticipating and correcting data-communications-network problems. So Ahlstrom and Lamarche went to work designing a computer display to show operators what parts of their systems were headed for trouble and needed attention. "The problem existed first," says Lamarche. "The product was created to meet the demand." The partners call their Mt. Laurel, New Jersey, company Avant-Garde Computing, Inc., and in fiscal 1984 it posted sales of $15.4 million, up from $1.5 million in 1981. Ahlstrom and Lamarche, incidentally, are still at it. Once a year they invite their customers in to hear about new products and play another round of the concept game.

Pre-Owned Business Concepts

While every business needs a concept, you don't necessarily have to figure one out for yourself.

Sometimes the idea for a new billion-dollar industry will present itself in the guise of something people are doing on the sly (with entrepreneurs catching on to what's happening months or even years later). This occurred a while back with bicycle motocross, or BMX, in which youngsters, from preschoolers on up, ride small, stripped-down, knobby-tired, lightweight bicycles around dirt tracks full of bumps and turns. The sport started quietly in Southern California more than ten years ago, when kids started sneaking into empty lots to play at being motorcycle daredevils.

Today, according to the Bicycle Manufacturers Association of America, 40 percent of all bikes sold in the United States are BMX models, with sales in 1984 reaching more than three million units, at a cost ranging from $65 to more than $1,000 apiece. Add to this the small fortune that young BMX enthusiasts' families can spend on a nylon racing suit ($90), fiberglass helmet ($75), special shoes ($30), and goggles ($20), not to mention admission fees to some six hundred BMX tracks around the country, or the cost of subscribing to glossy BMX magazines that have appeared out of nowhere—and you've got a new ten-figure industry that's produced quite a few seven-figure BMX moguls.

If consumers won't give you a concept free of charge, you can always rent one, or buy one outright.

You can rent a concept by paying a successful American company for the right to sell—and frequently make—its product, or you can import and distribute foreign products such as Scotch whiskey. You can buy a concept outright by purchasing the company that owns it, as Asa Chandler did in 1899 when he paid $2,300 for what would later become the Coca-Cola Company, whose 1984 sales topped $7 billion.

Hertz, Baskin-Robbins, McDonald's, and Holiday Inn are a few of the legendary business concepts available for rental, along with hundreds of others from greeting cards to computer stores. These companies deliver their concepts via a franchise agreement under which they promise to supply resources such as their product, the means to make their product, training, national advertising etc., which are essential to turning their concepts into successful businesses. You, on the other hand, pay the company an up-front franchise fee of anywhere from roughly $1,000 to over $500,000, in addition to supplying the capital to get the business going, perhaps some business experience, and the willingness to work gruelingly long hours turning your franchise into a money-maker.

"When you buy a franchise, you're starting a business from zero," says Andrew Kostecka, the top franchising expert at the U.S. Department of Commerce in Washington, D.C., "and you gotta work at that business, building it up. You gotta do everything. Clean the floors, put the lightbulbs in, run the books, hire the personnel, train 'em—everything. In the normal franchise business you're not going to make any money the first year. You're going to break even, if you're lucky. But then you start making money. Since nineteen fifty," says Kostecka, "franchising has created more millionaires than anything else."

The word *franchise* comes from the French *franchir,* which originally meant "to be free from servitude." Close to two thousand companies, many with instantly recognizable trademarks such as ComputerLand, Dunkin' Donuts, H&R Block, and Roto-Rooter, distribute their products, services, or methods through franchisees, and according to the Commerce Department they are expected to do a combined business of more than $529 billion in 1985, up from $112.8 billion in 1969. Today, franchising accounts for about 33 percent of all retail sales, and the Commerce Department predicts that by the year 2000 its share will hit 50 percent.

Some franchising companies, such as Duraclean International of Deerfield, Illinois, which shows franchisees how to set up their own carpet-and-upholstered-furniture-cleaning business, have been known to use a straightforward "fear pitch" in their advertising. "Before more jobs disappear through mergers, automation, and mechanization," warned one Duraclean ad, "shouldn't you at least investigate the way in which so many men have become owners of profitable businesses—starting in spare time—and independent of jobs, bosses, strikes, layoffs, and automation?"

Burger King is as good an example as any of what top-of-the-line franchisers will charge you to rent their concepts, and what you can expect in return. According to the company, "Burger King Corporation has an established minimum financial requirement for franchise applicants of a net worth of $200,000, of which $130,000 must be in liquid assets. It charges an initial franchise fee of $40,000, a royalty fee of 3.5 percent of gross sales, and 4 percent for advertising. If the land and building for the restaurant are leased from Burger King, the rent will be a minimum monthly rental or 8½ percent of annual gross sales, whichever is greater. Burger King considers factors in addition to financial strength when evaluating the qualifications of its applicants. These other requirements include management ability, people skills, leadership, and a commitment to operate the business for the term of the agreement. If an applicant is accepted as a Burger King franchisee—and less than 10 percent of the one-thousand-plus who apply each year are accepted—a total of six weeks training is required in a Burger King® restaurant, a regional training center, and at Burger King University in Miami. Only then will an applicant be ready to join Burger King Corporation's chain of four thousand restaurants, where average sales are in excess of $940,000."

Since the franchise industry has long been bedeviled by charlatans and fly-by-nighters, it pays to check out any franchise offer within an inch of its life, a job recently made easier by the Federal Trade Commission's ruling requiring all franchisers doing business across state lines to make a full financial disclosure to potential franchisees.

This disclosure statement forces franchisers, under penalty of the law, to provide information on critical facets of the business they're trying to get prospects to buy. Among them are the franchiser's business experience, previous bankruptcies if any, training program, site-selection assistance, territorial protection, supporting documentation for any earnings claims made to prospects, plus the percentage of existing franchisees who have actually achieved these results, and a list of the names and addresses of all the other franchisees.

"If you're going to spend $100,000 on a franchise, you'd better investigate before you invest," says the Commerce Department's Kostecka. "You'd better read the franchiser's disclosure document even though it's long and detailed. Pay particular attention to the company's financial statements, the experience of its officers, and get a list of as many of its franchisees as you can and contact both those that are happy and unhappy."

Money Machines for Sale

All successful businesses are moneymaking machines, and buying one outright is considerably riskier than purchasing a franchise unless you're already experienced in that business, or can get the owner to assume the role of a franchiser and stay on, holding your hand until you know what you're doing.

Newspapers are very often filled with advertisements for businesses for sale of every description: bars, beauty salons, restaurants, gas stations, laundromats, hotels, printing plants, lumberyards, even golf courses. The Sunday *New York Times* contains hundreds of these ads, from "Small downtown beauty salon nets $45K/yr. Asking $30K cash," to "Italian rest. Volume $10,000/wk. Price $140,000. Cash $45,000 down." The classified sections of *Inc.* and other entrepreneurially oriented magazines also contain ads for brokers who have businesses to sell, such as, "For Sale by Owner: 13,000 Businesses from Coast to Coast, No Brokerage Commission, Inquiries welcome."

Ron Hoglund, President of Sherwood's Commercial Brokers in St. Petersburg, Florida—the oldest and largest in the Sunshine State—says, "We have businesses for sale from $5,000 on up, and the more cash you're willing to put down, the better price you can get from the seller. The average seller will be willing to stay on for thirty days to teach you the business at no charge, but after that they'll want to be paid, or taken care of in some fashion.

"The first thing I would emphasize if you're going to buy a small business," says Hoglund, "is that you be ready to work. If you're going in with a lackadaisical attitude, or planning to work an eight-hour day, five days a week, then do yourself a favor and forget about buying a business. You should also have some money over and above what you're going to put down— in other words, some kind of backup for a rainy day, expansion, or whatever. The other thing you should establish is a good banking relationship. Most of the banks in this area are rather staid, but there are a few that are very aggressive and interested in the businessman. The last thing is, as soon as you get your business, train a relative, a close friend, or somebody in the organization you can trust to fill in for you in case of illness, a mishap, or the like."

It's interesting to note, by the way, the very different kinds of businesses that the nation's biggest corporations are buying these days as they attempt to position themselves for the future. Two examples: General Motors and R. J. Reynolds.

General Motors is buying into or acquiring outright companies in advanced-technology fields such as robotics, artificial intelligence, and data processing, not to mention a minuscule—for GM—investment in a tiny quality-control outfit called Philip Crosby Associates, headed by a man with whom we'll talk at length later in this book.

R. J. Reynolds, on the other hand, has acquired Kentucky Fried Chicken, which is the antithesis of high-tech, but has nevertheless enabled Reynolds to climb aboard not one, but three trends. And whenever you can go with the flow in business, do it.

The trends that Reynolds bought into were (1) the sharp increase in the number of women leaving home (and kitchen) and streaming into the paid labor force, (2) the resulting increase in households eating out, and (3) the nation's rising preference for chicken over beef.

Reynolds's purchase of Kentucky Fried Chicken, with its six thousand stores, gave it undisputed dominance of the $4.4-billion fast-food chicken market that's been growing at more than 20 percent a year recently, and has a lot more growth left in it than the $19-billion market for hamburgers that's 70-percent saturated and fiercely competitive.

This may help explain why Reynolds keeps the "secret recipe" for cooking Colonel Sanders' "finger-lickin' good" fried chicken—first sold at his Corbin, Kentucky, gas station in 1939—under eleven locks in a fireproof, bombproof vault at its corporate headquarters in Louisville.

When you've got a great concept, you look after it. When you've got one that's riding into the future on a trend, you treat it like the family jewels.

3

Scanning the Mysterious Future

"We live in turbulent times. Massive social and economic changes are underway, and those who opt for risk aversion are courting disaster."

—Thomas M. Loarie,
President,
Novacor Medical Corporation

Human beings have always been curious about the future. We've tossed bones, examined animal entrails, shuffled cards, peered into crystal balls, and prayed for divine revelation, all in an effort to prepare ourselves for things to come.

We would never have to be apprehensive about the future if we could prepare for tomorrow on the basis of what happened yesterday. But we can't, because, unlike our grandparents, we live in a world we ourselves made, and are aggressively re-making. As a result, today's U.S. economy is strewn with the bones of failed entrepreneurs who lacked a vision of America's kaleidoscopically changing future. The victims range from bankrupt real-estate developers zapped by rampaging interest rates to out-of-work filling-station owners bushwhacked by OPEC price increases, collapsing gasoline sales, and self-service price-cutters.

To be in business during the waning years of the twentieth century is to be engulfed by change, by events both unforeseen and unfamiliar, from the rise of politically powerful environmentalists (and more recently evangelical Christians) to the quantum leaps in energy prices, the coming of the Information Age, and the seminal shift currently under way from a managerial to an entrepreneurial economy.

The rest of this century will undoubtedly witness other breaks with the past: possibly the announcement of antigravity technology, severe climatic changes endangering America's agricultural heartland, nuclear terrorism, or even the sudden emergence of an irresistible worldwide outcry for disarmament and peace.

The upshot of all this is that if you want to reduce the risk of being blindsided by change, you must keep your antennae up, carefully examining the forces reshaping America's future before launching a new business, and continually scanning the future for clues to new trends once you're in business.

"In the current environment of rapid technological and social change," says Richard S. Hickok, chairman of the American Institute of CPAs' future-issues committee, "the traditional approach of reacting to developments on an ad hoc basis is no longer workable. What is needed is a practical, organized system to anticipate threats and opportunities and to decide what to do about them."*

The lack of such a system caught Levi Strauss flatfooted when it missed the threat buried in the aging of the "baby boom" generation, whose middle-aged spread has cooled its infatuation with blue jeans. The rush of women into the paid labor force, on the other hand, has created an unprecedented opportunity for entrepreneurs such as Lillian Vernon Katz, who recognized the need of these busy women to do more of their shopping from home. The direct-marketing business that Mrs. Katz started in 1951 at age twenty-three, when she bought a $495 ad in *Seventeen* magazine offering a monogrammed

---

*Richard S. Hickok, "Looking to the Future: A Key to Success," *Journal of Accountancy* (March 1984):77.

belt and pocketbook, has grown into a catalog company grossing $100 million a year.

Peering into Tomorrow

Among the best ways to scan the mysterious future for trends that could help or hurt your business are to:

Widen your reading. It was by perusing two million newspaper articles over a twelve-year period that John Naisbitt uncovered the "Ten New Directions Transforming Our Lives" described in *Megatrends*. Spot-checking special-interest publications can also alert you to trends months ahead of their appearance in the mainstream media. The vitamin and nutrition craze, for instance, came as no surprise to even casual readers of *Prevention* magazine.

Talk to strangers. There are people who look at things through spectacles very different from yours. An hour's chat with a welfare mother, computer hacker, handicapped person, or someone a generation older or younger than you are can expand your entire world-view. Coin-operated-game manufacturers paid dearly for their intellectual insularity in 1972 when they rejected videogame developer Nolan Bushnell's offer to put them into the most lucrative new entertainment product their industry had ever seen. The reason? The coin-op men were living in the fading electromechanical era and had never been exposed to a character like Bushnell, who epitomized the onrushing age of electronics.*

Think through the second, third, and nth-order consequences of events. As Garrett Hardin, professor emeritus of Human Ecology at the University of California, Santa Barbara,

*Scott Cohen, *ZAP The Rise and Fall of ATARI* (New York: McGraw-Hill, 1984), 31.

reminds us, "We can never do just one thing." Henry Ford had no idea that his "tin lizzie" would change America into a drive-thru culture where people could eat, shop, bank, worship, procreate, and view their departed loved ones without ever leaving their vehicles.

There's probably no better way to start building the data base you'll need to scan the future than by grounding yourself in three of the most fundamental trends currently reshaping America, which no entrepreneur can afford to ignore:

- the troubled U.S. economy
- the graying of the American consumer
- the technological tidal wave sweeping us all from the Industrial Age to the Information Age

In a talk to the Executives' Club of Chicago, John B. Fery, chairman and chief executive officer of the $3.8-billion Boise Cascade Corporation, drew a disturbing picture of the United States economic outlook during the years ahead. "Ours is the Age of Uncertainty," said Fery. "We know the economy is evolving, but we don't know to what. We could be in the beginning of a long period of disinflation," said Fery, "with slow growth and tremendous pressure on interest rates. That sounds likely to many. Or the tremendous pressure on interest rates could result in another firestorm of inflation . . . or recession . . . or both. Those are fearful possibilities. Or we could be in the midst of a lengthy economic transition of a kind we can't define. That may be the most frightening scenario of all."

While the precise gravity of the nation's economic outlook is a matter of conjecture, the graying of American consumers is a demographic certainty.

Old Folks and Baby-Boomers

Americans born in 1982 can expect to live a record 74.6 years, according to the latest detailed study by the National Center for Health Statistics. And projections released by the Census Bureau in 1984 indicate that by the year 2050 there will be more Americans sixty-five and older than eighteen and younger, and that by 2080 these senior citizens will represent almost a quarter of the U.S. population. "American life once ended at an average age of fifty. Soon, middle age will begin at fifty," says National Medical Enterprises, a Los Angeles-based $2-billion-plus health care giant specializing in "extending and enhancing the human life span."

The elderly market is already an entrepreneur's dream, according to Fabian Linden, executive director of the Consumer Research Center at the Conference Board in New York, a leading business-supported research institution.

"When you go into the older segment of the population," says Linden, "you get a triple bang. Number one, you get a higher average income than you do with the young. Number two, you get a much higher per capita income, since the family size is contracting when the younger people's is expanding. And, number three, there are more older people than there are younger people. Over and above all this, of course, is the fact that if you're thirty you're worrying about sending your kids to college, buying appliances for the home, clothes for your back, and everything else. But when you get to a certain age, all these things are there. All the durables, the mortgage on the home has probably been paid off—older people are simply a better bet."

Linden then backs this up with figures from a joint study that the Conference Board recently completed with the Census Bureau, titled *A Marketer's Guide to Discretionary Income.* "Households headed by persons 30 to 34," says Linden, "have an average after-tax income of $16,959 compared with people

50 to 55, who have $20,423, and those 55 to 60, who have $19,123. What's really incredible," says Linden, "is that those 65 and older have a higher after-tax per capita income than all age groups under the age of 50."

The most fascinating aspect of the "graying of America" is the fact that the highly publicized "baby boom" generation is nearing middle age. More and more of the Americans born from 1946 through 1964—one-third of our present population—are moving into their thirties, a vast army of well-educated, well-heeled consumers. As this legion of baby-boomers has traveled through the postwar years, it has generated a huge, moving, pig-in-a-python demand for everything from pacifiers to prophylactics, and those who saw the baby-boomers coming profited handsomely.

People Weekly magazine, which credits the baby-boomers for its phenomenal success, launched an advertising campaign in 1984 whose tag line was *"People:* We're Booming." Headlined *People's* first ad in *The New York Times*: "Johnny's Grown Up. He's looking for a new set of wheels." Any day now, Johnny's going to join the 36 million Americans who wear eyeglasses, pushing the total up to an estimated 59 million by the year 2000. And not long after that, Johnny will be in the market for a hearing aid.

Jeff Dahlberg, president of a Golden Valley, Minnesota, company that manufactures hearing aids and is franchising walk-in Miracle Ear Centers to sell them, estimates that 17 million Americans need these tiny battery-powered devices, which can be customized to fit unobtrusively within the ear at a cost of about $1,000.

As today's baby-boomers advance toward Golden Pond—they'll all get there by 2030, when the last ones turn 65—it will force some companies to change their strategies, while other, better-positioned ones can simply sit back and enjoy. The nation's theme parks, for example, are already emphasizing the mature delights of good food, attractive merchandise, and big-name entertainment, as well as stomach-wrenching roller-coaster rides.

One entrepreneur who went all the way to investigate the elderly market is Patricia Moore, who heads her own New York research and design firm, and at twenty-six years of age transformed herself into an eighty-five-year-old woman by using mild saline solution to blur her vision, putty to impair her hearing, elastic bandages to stiffen her joints, and a professional makeup artist to add wrinkles and white hair.

During the next few years, masquerading as an elderly American, Moore shopped, visited government agencies catering to the needs of older people, and talked to senior citizens in 116 cities. She was mugged by a group of boys in New York City, shunned by Yuppie professionals attending a gerontology conference in Columbus, Ohio, and had pebbles thrown at her by children in Clearwater, Florida.

Moore used the lessons she learned on these trips to advise clients such as American Express and IBM on how to attract elderly consumers. Among her suggestions: use easy-to-read type on product labels and brochures, consider using Velcro fasteners on clothes instead of tough-to-manipulate hooks and buttons, make sure containers are easy to open (child-proof drug packages can also be elderly-proof), provide two-handle coffee cups for people suffering from Parkinson's disease, and always make sure there's seating available for older customers if they have to wait for something like a drug prescription to be filled. "If your business is sensitive to the needs of elderly consumers," says Moore, "that's where they will flock."

The Fourth Industrial Revolution

The moneymaking possibilities inherent in America's aging population are refreshingly predictable. Forecasting the future of science and technology, however, has always been hazardous, and never more so than today, as we move into what Dr.

George Kozmetsky, co-founder of Los Angeles' $3.5-billion Teledyne, Inc., and director of the Institute for Constructive Capitalism at the University of Texas at Austin, calls the Fourth Industrial Revolution.

Dr. Kozmetsky believes the United States and the world's other industrialized nations have reached their present state of economic well-being by moving up through three increasingly sophisticated levels of technology, based on (1) manufacturing textiles, making iron from coke, and supplying power from Watt's steam engine, (2) railroads and steelmaking, and (3) electricity, batch chemicals, and the internal-combustion engine.

Now, says Kozmetsky, we are moving into the Fourth Industrial Revolution, which is based on microelectronics, biotechnology, lasers, artificial intelligence and robotics, synthetic materials, waste technologies, and communications.

"These and other innovations in the next few decades," says Dr. Kozmetsky, "will lead to markets for advanced materials, special-application designs, photosynthesis, supercold technology, industrial and scientific instrumentation, robots, and automated batch and process production. All of these Fourth Industrial Revolution technologies should lead to long-term investments in newer plants and equipment, increased productivity, and a stronger U.S. international trade posture."

There are four fairly obvious ways that even the smallest entrepreneur can cash in on the high-tech revolution bursting out of the world's research and development laboratories.

Using high-tech tools to boost efficiency and profits. Pocket calculators, office copiers, telephone-answering machines, and other devices we take for granted today are continually being joined by more advanced electronic helpmates, of which the computer is by far the most significant. San Francisco's Wine and Cheese Center, which does well over $1 million worth of business a year, selling some 200 different kinds of cheeses,

400 different wines, and dozens of crackers and snacks, couldn't live without its computer, according to store manager Roger Moore. The computer allows Wine and Cheese to:

- Keep track of what's selling, and what's gathering dust.
- Immediately update prices on the hundreds of items available on the store's shelves. (Wine and Cheese's fifteen full-time and five part-time employees couldn't do this before the computer was brought in, leading management to think its poor margins were the result of stealing instead of out-of-date pricing.)
- Automate its customer charge accounts, thereby sharply reducing billing problems.
- Automate its accounts payable, general ledger, and customer mailing list, which can now be sorted by name, Zip Code, and so on.
- Offer its customers help in selecting the right wine for their meals by using a computer terminal they can operate themselves, located right next to the wine rack.

Serving the needs of high-tech companies. America's highest-tech superstars, from the gene-splicing Genentech to the robot-making Unimation, need highly specialized materials, from data-carrying fiber optics to data-processing 256K microchips, which only a handful of companies can supply. But they also need more mundane stuff such as stationery, cleaning services, and insurance, which are the traditional preserve of small local vendors.

One of the most effervescent businesswomen I've met recently is Kay Taylor, who was running the Little Dipper Fondue and Specialty Restaurant in Melbourne, Florida, when a construction crew building a shopping center across the street asked her to bring them some fast food. Today, Kay owns four trucks delivering meals to high-tech industrial parks near the Kennedy Space Center, the Warehouse Deli which serves sit-down meals at another park, and a catering service. Together they grossed $500,000 in 1984.

The big challenge for small firms, of course, is to supply high-tech companies' more esoteric and hence more profitable needs, such as the protection of proprietary information, which is rapidly becoming a matter of life and death for many high-tech corporations.

Getting a toehold in a high-tech business. Advancing technology has created more small U.S. businesses than anything else, with today's ubiquitous copy centers, computer stores, and videogame parlors following in the footsteps of other enterprises fathered by the automobile, farm equipment, sewing machines, and similar inventions. There are countless ways for entrepreneurs to enter the high-tech age:

- If you own a personal-service business, such as a candy store or a barber shop, consider adding some high-tech hardware to boost your profits. Quite a few candy stores are reaping a harvest of quarters with video games, and a barber in Chicago saw his business take off after he started offering parents a free video tape of Junior getting his first haircut.
- If you're intrigued by a piece of advanced technology, consider building a business around it. A friend of mine bought a cheap Radio Shack computer to help him manage his construction business, and is now working full time—and making a lot more money—showing other builders how to use computers to manage theirs.
- If you know someone you respect who is planning to start up a high-tech business, consider investing some of your time, know-how, services, or money in the enterprise. A man I know who runs a small nursery acted as marketing consultant to a friend of his, who had started a little company making solar-powered water distillers.
- If you're lucky, you may even get a technological boost without doing anything. The advent of nonstop music television (MTV), featuring rock stars dressed in the latest fashions,

helped send the sales of the super-trendy Merry-Go-Round clothing chain, headquartered in Towson, Maryland, through the roof.

Counterbalancing high-tech with no-tech. In *Megatrends,* John Naisbitt advances a formula he calls "high tech/high touch" to describe one result of the headlong rush into the Information Age. "What happens," says Naisbitt, "is that whenever new technology is introduced into society, there must be a counterbalancing human response—that is, *high touch*—or the technology is rejected." He adds, "We must learn to balance the material wonders of technology with the spiritual demands of our human nature."

As we are forced to process more and more data in order to survive in the high-tech Information Age, we are understandably reaching out for products and services that remind us of what it's like to be a sensual, flesh-and-blood human being rather than a mere synapse in America's increasingly wired society. This is opening up a whole new window of opportunity for entrepreneurial energy, whose future course no one can predict—although there are clues:

- Linda Mendelson, a knitter from Yonkers, New York, makes colorful, handmade sweaters and other "wearable art" clothes, frequently incorporating lines of verse from Emily Dickinson, Walt Whitman, and other poets. These items are suitable for hanging on the wall as decorations when they're not being worn.
- Birthing centers where women can have their babies delivered by midwives in homelike surroundings, instead of high-tech, high-priced hospital delivery rooms, are increasing by leaps and bounds.
- Jim Sanford has built a nice business by holding old-fashioned, New England–style clambakes on his Manhattan clients' apartment balconies and penthouse roofs. Sanford says he feels "very fortunate to be making a living doing

something I truly enjoy." He also makes about as much money during the June-to-October clambake season as he did working year-round as a chef for someone else, allowing him to winter in Egypt, Indonesia, Thailand, and other far-away places.

For the rest of this century, and well into the next, economic activity growing out of Information Age technology will be on a growth trajectory, along with other less hardware-rich businesses designed to satisfy the hunger of the human heart.

A working knowledge of the economic, demographic, and technological changes reshaping America is essential if you hope to make it in a business of your own.

4

Changing Paper into Gold

"Most first-time entrepreneurs don't know what they need or how to get it."

—Donald de Renne,
Partner,
Emprise Management

Once you've got a business concept firmly in mind, and are convinced it will be helped rather than hurt by whatever changes you see reshaping America's future, then you're ready to begin work on your business plan.

Just about the most important thing you can do to turn your new business idea into a moneymaking reality is to prepare this step-by-step strategy, describing exactly how you plan to pull it off.

This means thinking through the product you're going to sell, the resources you'll need to make and market it, how you propose to obtain these resources, the money you'll make, and how much you'll have left over as profit after all the bills have been paid.

The next step is to reduce all this information to numbers detailing the costs involved in turning out your product, as well as the sales and profits you believe it will generate. The final step is to convert this data into a pro forma or "best guess" profit-and-loss statement showing your business's outgo and income every year for three to five years, and a balance sheet predicting where its assets and liabilities will stand at the end of each of these years.

The Other Bottom Line

A well-thought-out business plan can be worth infinitely more than its weight in gold, so it will pay you to assemble yours with considerable care. And when you do, don't forget to think about your personal goals in life—what a recent article in *Working Woman* magazine rightly called "The Other Bottom Line."

Working Woman quotes Marjorie Walker, a principal of the Center for Business Planning in Weston, Massachusetts, who believes that if you're thinking about going into business for yourself, you should "be realistic about who you are and what you want from life." Among the questions you should ask yourself, says Ms. Walker, are:

What is your commitment to the business? Is it merely an extension of a hobby, something you hope will bring in a little extra money, or are you willing to make a significant financial and time commitment, even to the extent of adversely affecting your life-style?

How hard do you want to work? Do you think having your own business will free up time for fun and family, or do you understand that nearly all businesses that eventually become lucrative will require large expenditures of energy, especially in the business's formative years?

Will your family back you up? There's nothing more discouraging than trying to run a business and having a spouse in the background disparaging the effort.

Where do you want to be in three to five years? Do you want a nice little business providing you with a comfortable living, or a fast-growing one with employees and managerial challenge? Or perhaps something in between?

My first hands-on experience with putting together a business plan occurred in the late sixties, when a twenty-seven-year-old ball of fire named Howard Meyers asked me to help him raise the $750,000 in equity money and $1,356,000 in long-term-debt money that he needed to buy and upgrade the Revere Smelting & Refining Corporation of Newark, New Jersey, which was in the scrap-metal recycling business. Meyers had been in this business since he was twenty, he knew Revere and its aging owners very well, and during a six-month period when he managed the company for them, he had increased its after-tax profits from $16,671 to $41,076.

The financial community had never heard of Howard Meyers, yet he had worked out such a convincing business plan for turning the barely profitable Revere into a real money-maker that he had little trouble finding the capital he needed to buy the business, replace its old 9,000-ton-a-year recycling plant with a technologically advanced 24,000-ton facility, or achieve the surging profits projected in his five-year financial statements.

The Dead-Battery Business

Meyers's business plan for Revere started out by telling the story of the company's unusual business, which consisted of buying old car batteries, electrical cable, and other scrap from dealers in New Jersey, New York, and southern New England, breaking it up, and then smelting it down into unrefined "hogs" of reclaimed metal. Dealers were paid for the amount of lead in their scrap, multiplied by its current market price, less a fee that Revere charged for converting it into lead ingots. Revere made its money from these fees, plus its charge for alloying this lead with antimony, tin, and other nonferrous metals that its customers then used to make new car batteries, ammunition, collapsible tubes, and other products. These valuable alloying metals are found as "impurities" in the scrap that Revere buys, and since industry custom is to pay dealers only for their scrap's lead content, Revere got those costly metals absolutely free.

Meyers's business plan said Revere had more than forty-five customers, including Exide, Remington Arms, American Can, and Grumman Aircraft, and that no one of them accounted for more than 16 percent of its output. The plan then went on to quote a Lead Industries Association report predicting that the secondary lead market was about to enjoy a decade of steady if modest growth, and to assert that Revere would not only share in this long-term growth, but would also profit from some near-term growth opportunities resulting from the demise of several competitors, along with a stepped-up marketing program.

Meyers noted that one of Revere's major competitors had recently gone out of business, that a second one had just been purchased by a large corporation that would probably soak up most of its output, and that a third's capacity was unlikely to be expanded to meet this new demand because of labor problems and space limitations on its existing production site.

Meyers said he thought he could grab some of this business for Revere, even though its old 9,000-ton smelting plant was already operating twenty-four hours a day, seven days a week. He said he had recently raised the plant's capacity some 7 percent by improving operating efficiencies, and that he had started buying already smelted hogs of secondary lead, which enabled Revere to sign its first contract with General Motors' battery-producing Delco-Remy Division, who had been buying from Revere's competitors. Meyers said there was other new business in the offing from Revere's present customers, who were expanding their production facilities, from the possibility of signing a long-term contract with a major battery manufacturer to salvage the lead from its old batteries, and by selling to new customers such as DuPont, which used large tonnages of secondary lead in the manufacture of tetraethyl lead gasoline additive, and was already doing business with Revere through DuPont's Remington Arms subsidiary. The business plan also noted that Revere was currently shipping fifty tons of secondary lead a month to Puerto Rico and Japan through Port Newark, within a stone's throw of its plant, and that it felt it could greatly increase its overseas business once its new 24,000-ton plant came on line.

Meyers's business plan stressed the fact that Revere's new plant would not only raise its output by more than 250 percent, but that its capacity could easily be increased to 36,000, 48,000, or 78,000 tons to keep pace with new customer demand. What's more, he said, the new plant would reduce Revere's production costs by 15 percent, making it one of the lowest-cost secondary lead producers in the United States, if not *the* lowest. While Revere planned to keep the 9,000-ton plant in production until the new 24,000-ton plant was completed, Meyers said some $125,000 worth of movable equipment from the old plant would be usable in the new one.

The new plant's smelting furnaces, Meyers said, would be able to process nearly three times as much scrap, with no increase in manpower. Fuel costs per ton of smelted metal would be decreased, and by introducing new fuels, the plant's output could be increased from 24,000 to as much as 30,000 tons a year. An atomic adsorption spectrometer would permit greater quality control. New mechanical casting machines would allow two men to do what it currently took five men to do. New materials-handling equipment would permit one man to load a truck with finished ingots faster than two men could do it at that time. The new plant's pollution-control system, Meyers went on to say, would cost about $300,000, but would trap almost all of the flue dust emitted by the plant, which contained 60 percent lead and would be cheaply recycled automatically, thus avoiding double handling of the material. It was expected that the value of the recovered lead would pay for the equipment in three to four years, after which it would begin making a contribution to profits.

Meyers's business plan also spelled out agreements he had negotiated with various local government bodies in Newark to get four acres of prime industrial land on which to build Revere's new plant at a knockdown price, a fifteen-year tax concession for building the new plant in Port Newark, and a special condemnation award of close to $450,000 for the old facilities it planned to tear down.

Meyers then turned to the most critical question of all—the management team that would be responsible for transforming Revere Smelting & Refining into the highly profitable, fast-growing company promised in his business plan.

Meyers listed biographical sketches of the seven most important members of his team, beginning with himself as president and a director; a young thirty-four-year-old metallurgical engineer who had managed one of the nation's largest nonferrous smelting companies as executive vice-president and a director; a fifty-one-year-old engineer who was a member of the selling family and an officer of Revere—and who would thus provide management continuity—as vice-president of production and a director; and a twenty-eight-year-old quality-control supervisor for a major company in the aircraft industry as director of quality control. Meyers's team was rounded out by Revere's retiring president and major owner, who would serve as a consultant and director, and a thirty-two-year-old lawyer and a twenty-nine-year-old CPA, who would serve as directors.

There was only one more critical piece to Meyers's business plan, and that was the four-year projected-income statement and balance sheet. This four-year spread sheet contained several hundred numbers, but the ones that most vividly summed up what Meyers thought he could do if he got his hands on Revere were sales rising from $4,180,000 in the first year after he took over to $15,200,000 in the fourth year, and all-important net income soaring from $47,000 in the first year to $600,000 in the fourth year of Meyers's reign. And even these figures might be conservative, Meyers's business plan noted, since they were projected on the basis of Revere getting $60 for smelting a ton of lead scrap, whereas the current industry rate was actually $75 a ton.

One of the first venture capitalists to see the possibility in Meyers's business plan for Revere was Alan Patricof, who was just starting in business himself, managing money for the Bloomingdales, Bronfmans, Wymans, and other well-to-do New York families. Patricof gave Meyers $450,000 of the money he needed to buy Revere in exchange for about 40 percent of the company. This was Patricof's first venture deal; he quadrupled his original investment as Meyers built Revere into a Dallas-based metals conglomerate that posted after-tax profits of $7.2 million on sales of $182.1 million just nine years after he put it together.

A carefully thought-out business plan should alert you to the mass of problems that must be solved if your business is to succeed. Failure to comprehend the nuances of the business you're about to enter, or to allow for the crises that will inevitably follow, could end in disaster.

Losing the Class Struggle

Bertell Ollman, Marxist professor of political science at New York University, learned this lesson the hard way not long after he had assembled a dozen or so friends in his Greenwich Village apartment and, over a brunch of lox and bagels, attempted to sell them on investing in a new business whose sole product was a board game called Class Struggle, in which

Capitalists grapple with Workers for survival. The game came packed in a box with a photograph of Nelson Rockefeller arm-wrestling Karl Marx on the cover.

Professor Ollman had done a little research into the game business, but as he sorrowfully recounts in his book *Class Struggle Is the Name of the Game,* he didn't do nearly enough, which sealed the company's fate from the outset. Only after he started making Class Struggle did he learn that 95 percent or more of the 300 to 400 new board games introduced each year never make it. He was even more surprised to discover that toy stores demanded a 50-percent discount off the manufacturer's list price (he thought it was only 33 percent), and that bad debts were a deadly problem in the game business (he was left holding the bag on more than $30,000 worth of unpaid bills, including one owed by a customer doing business under the name "Do Something for Jesus").

Ollman labored for four years on Class Struggle, and if he and his investors are lucky, they'll get their money back one day from royalties that continue to dribble in from the U.S. and abroad.

Another entrepreneur zapped by inadequate planning was Lance Weddell, who owns a company in Frankford, Maine, that manufactures survival equipment for hunters. Weddell came to grief when he decided to diversify into a new survival business—procuring hearts, livers, kidneys, and other organs from cadavers for sale to customers in need of transplants.

Weddell's Medical Lifeline, Inc., planned to make money by charging organ donors and recipients a fee of $40 to register with the firm, and by earning interest on the $10,000 that potential recipients were asked to leave on deposit for eventual payment to the estates of organ donors.

Weddell did get 267 potential donors to send in $40 registration fees, and five prospective organ recipients called to inquire about the firm's services, although none of them sent in $10,000. The gap in Weddell's business plan, which was to close down Medical Lifeline just five months after it opened its doors, was that he couldn't get physicians to remove purchased organs from his donors. Commercializing organ transplants violated their code of medical ethics.*

Lance Weddell had neglected to do his homework, which can condemn any new business to Death Row. Take the great digital watch disaster of the seventies, for example. Here was a business that had everything. An eye-stopping new way to tell time based on the latest in microchip technology, constantly falling prices, and the undivided attention of more than twenty of the nation's most self-assured microchip manufacturers.

Yet, as Dirk Hanson reveals in *The New Alchemists: Silicon Valley and the Microelectronics Revolution,* most of these chip manufacturers lost their shirts on digital watches. The reason? They didn't do their homework. The chip makers were superb at making and marketing chips, but they didn't know the first thing about selling watches, which have more to do with jewelry, apparel, and cosmetics than with electronics. The chip makers were also ignorant of the Madison Avenue–style advertising needed to sell watches, of the industry's chaotic pricing policies, or of its peculiar business cycle, in which most of its inventory moves during the few weeks before Christmas. "Inventories were a shambles," says Hanson, "prices were almost whimsically malleable, and as for matters of styling, packaging design, shelf placement, and TV spots, chip makers proved to be true babes in the woods."

The $5-Million Brainstorm

Contrast the experiences of Ollman, Weddell, and the chip makers with the flawless way that Donald Massaro and David

---

*Fern Schumer Chapman, "The Life-and-Death Question of an Organ Market," *Fortune* (June 11, 1984):108–118.

Liddle started up Metaphor Computer Systems of Mountain View, California, so that its success—and their considerable fortunes—were virtually assured even before they began doing business in 1983.

Massaro and Liddle were well-known executives of the Xerox Corporation, with impressive credentials in office automation systems, when they quit out of frustration to form Metaphor.

Massaro came to Xerox in 1978 when it bought Shugart Associates, a maker of computer disk drives. Massaro had been named president of Shugart in 1974, the year it lost $2.5 million. But by the time Xerox bought it four years later, Massaro had turned Shugart into a money-maker with nearly $100 million in sales.

Xerox put Massaro in charge of its office-products division, whose sales he quickly increased from $200 million to $500 million. The division never made money, however, and Massaro soon found himself in basic disagreement with Xerox's conservative marketing strategies.

Liddle, Metaphor's other founder, worked at Xerox's Palo Alto Research Center, where an idea he had for a new office product was backed by Xerox management, but never given a chance to fly in the marketplace. It was at this point that Liddle and Massaro decided to incorporate Metaphor and strike out on their own.

Massaro and Liddle figured there were thousands of managers whose jobs depended on having quick access to information stored in their companies' big IBM computers, but who couldn't get at it because they didn't know how to program these machines to do what they wanted them to do. As a result, they were at the mercy of their companies' data-processing departments, which were usually far too busy to offer them meaningful help.

Metaphor's brainstorm was to design an easy-to-use, reasonably priced office work station for these managers, one whose built-in programming would be tailored to their specific needs so they could get into their companies' IBM computers whenever they wished.

Metaphor estimated that there were 113,500 managers out of 22 million white-collar professionals who were prime prospects for its work stations. And to reach them it decided to set up its own direct-sales force concentrated in just three cities, where it believed 75 to 80 percent of these target users were located. Metaphor's new business concept was so beautifully thought out, and the reputations of Massaro and Liddle were so bankable, that when they approached the San Francisco venture-capital firm of Hambrecht & Quest for $500,000 to develop a more detailed business plan, they were given $5 million instead and told to get started.

Not far from Metaphor Computer Systems in Mountain View, California, is the Palo Alto Brewery, one of the new "microbreweries" that have bubbled up in recent years to produce a relatively few barrels of specialized beers a day for limited distribution (compared to the 170,000 barrels per day that Anheuser-Busch pumps out).

The brewery belongs to Kenneth Kolence, co-founder of one of the Silicon Valley's first successful computer software companies, and his son Jeffery, who began planning the brewery while studying plant engineering at the California Polytechnical Institute.

Jeffery's senior paper at Cal Poly examined how the physical plants of micro-breweries were organized, along with the business mistakes made by those still in production. After analyzing Jeffery's data, the Kolences decided there was money to be made in micro-brewing, and set up Handcrafted Beer, Inc., to deal themselves into the game.

The next step in developing the game plan was deciding on the kind of beer to produce. The Kolences had been impressed by U.S. Census reports showing that California had both the highest per capita sales of imported beer and the greatest number of Britishers of any state in the Union, so they decided to brew a traditional, unpasteurized English dark beer known as "bitter."

While Kenneth Kolence set about raising the $400,000 of capital called for in the game plan, young Jeff traveled to the Fremlins Brewery in Faversham, England, near Canterbury, to take an intensive six-week course in how to run a small brewery.

Jeff had no sooner completed the course than he set off in search of the perfect English beer to copy, eventually settling on a brand called Brakspears Best Bitter, of Henley-on-Thames. Jeff next selected England's Edme's Malting House to supply his brewery with malt, and Inn Brewing Ltd. to custom-make the equipment to brew his product, which he named London Real Ale. Jeff then returned to California, rented a 2,000-square-foot building to house his brewery, and set up a system of water purifiers to supply it with the U.S. equivalent of the legendary brewing waters of England's Burton-Upon-Trent district.

The Kolences' brewery equipment, along with a supply of malt, hops, and kegs, arrived in California on October 7, 1983, and a week later the first keg of London Real Ale was tapped. By the end of 1984 the five-man brewery was running nearly flat out, shipping more than seventy-five U.S. barrels of London Real Ale a week to customers in the San Francisco Bay area. Sometime toward the end of 1985, the Kolences expect to be shipping 200 barrels a week, which would net them a nice little profit in addition to all the fun they're having in the brewery business.

The Kolences beautifully illustrate the importance of research when developing a business plan: interviewing people already in the business you're going to enter, making the rounds of prospective customers (do they need what you're planning to sell? do they have any special likes or dislikes? how much are they willing to pay?), studying the competition, lining up suppliers, checking out places to house the business, talking to potential employees, arranging sources of financing, and the like. This process can take anywhere from a few weeks to several years, but if you're thinking about going into business for yourself, you couldn't make a better investment.

"It's always interesting to me to see someone write a business plan and watch thousands or millions of dollars come rushing in on a piece of paper," says Dr. Joseph R. Mancuso, president of New York's Center for Entrepreneurial Management, who writes and lectures extensively about how to prepare and present a winning business plan.

Five Golden Minutes

"Good business plans are like good stories, like interesting articles in *Business Week*," says Mancuso. "The trouble is that they're seldom written for the reader. Instead, they're written by people who need to clear their souls, to tell it all, or because they want to drop some data. They think a venture capitalist is going to take seven days reading their plan. What they don't realize is that it's the first five minutes their business plan is in a reader's hands that's golden. This is when the guy's going to say, 'Hey, this looks good, I'll read it all.'

"There's no standard format for a business plan any more than there's a standard format for a piece of art. I've seen some very successful five-page plans. The key thing is to show how you're going to go from here to there over time. I always suggest getting some outside help. In every major city there are a hundred people that make a living doing business plans, and most of them charge between $5,000 and $10,000. I would suggest doing a plan all the way through to the end, and then let somebody else polish it. And remember, raising capital is the art of reducing risks, not selling dreams.

"And don't get dejected if your plan is turned down. Every single business plan I've ever seen got turned down initially. Digital Equipment Corporation, one of the most successful capital deals of all time, was turned down by everyone before American Research & Development finally put in some money. You should go into a venture capitalist's office seeking a 'no'; you should work hard to get a 'no,' because you can learn from negative feedback, and when you see the next venture capitalist he'll give you a 'maybe.' And before you know it you're getting yeses. You can write a business plan that's so good it will raise too much capital, and you'll have to make the agonizing, gut-wrenching decision of who you're going to have to cut out of the deal. Cetus got overfinanced, so did Storage Technology, and in the beginning *Venture* magazine had more potential investors than it needed. On a scale of one to ten, I call that an eleven."

5

Shaking the Money Tree

"An insufficiently capitalized organization will die—good and bad alike."

—Peter J. Boni,
President,
Summa Four

Scott Curtis is an ebullient forty-four-year-old mechanic who fixes up French-built Citroën automobiles in Santa Clara, California, calls his garage the Curtis Circus and himself the "head clown," sports a Frenchman's blue beret with his grease-stained overalls, and starts work in the morning by telling everyone within earshot, "It's going to be another wonderful Citroën day."

But what's really fascinating about Scott Curtis is that his little automobile repair and restoration business has been flourishing while the U.S. automobile industry has been fighting for its life against the Japanese, who have dethroned the United States as the world's leading manufacturer of motorcars.

Which raises the question of what Scott Curtis knows that Detroit doesn't. The answer is that he's

• meeting today's consumer demand for longer-lasting products;

- cutting product costs by using "remanufactured" old parts with years of useful life still left in them;
- saving customers money by involving them in product maintenance;
- building a four-star reputation for excellence, which these days can enable even the smallest business to create a demand for its work among customers virtually anywhere in the world.

Curtis got into business for himself the way many entrepreneurs do—he worked a regular nine-to-five job that paid the rent, with a little left over to buy the tools and other equipment he needed to begin repairing Citroëns on the side. This is a prudent way to finance a business, since if it goes down the drain, you've still got a way to earn your living.

"There's Money Out There"

But if you want to give your new business everything you've got (with no distractions), then you'll most likely end up financing it with personal assets, money from family and friends, loans from banks and other institutions, high-risk money advanced by venture capitalists who'll want a big piece of your hide in return, or even by selling stock to the investing public, if you can convince an underwriter that you've got a hot concept. "Entrepreneurs are saying, 'There's money out there and some of it's got my name on it,'" says Stanley E. Pratt, publisher of the *Venture Capital Journal.*

Scott Curtis got started on the road to a business of his own back in high school, when he became hooked on cars. He worked part-time for a Rolls-Royce mechanic, sweeping the man's floors and cleaning his tools in return for getting a solid basic education in automotive repair.

Gradually, Curtis became interested in having a small automobile-repair business of his own. He sent away for bro-

71

chures on small business, took any courses he could find, and, while enrolled at Foothill Junior College in Los Altos, had the good fortune to find "one incredible professor" who taught him just about everything he needed to know to get started.

It was while studying at Foothill that Curtis fell in love with the Citroën. The father of a girl he knew had one and asked him if he'd like to chauffeur his family to Salt Lake City and back in it. "I was so impressed by that car I couldn't believe it," says Curtis. "We cruised at 75 to 80 miles an hour, with five people plus baggage. The car rode like a dream and got 32 to 35 miles per gallon."

Curtis continued pursuing his studies at Heald's Business School in San Francisco, and after graduation he spent four years working as an audiovisual specialist at Foothill Junior College. He was making $620 a month gross in 1967, and could "have stayed there until I rotted." What saved him from that fate was that he had gotten into the business of fixing up Citroëns. "I'd get home from Foothill at 5:30 P.M.," he says, "grab a bite to eat, and work on a Citroën in the carport of our apartment until midnight."

Curtis kept planning ahead for the day when he'd own a car-repair business, which led him to the Citroën dealership in Palo Alto, where he talked the sales manager into letting him demonstrate cars to prospects he'd bring into the showroom. Curtis never asked for a penny in sales commissions, even though he figures ten to fifteen of his prospects ended up buying new cars. "What I wanted," says Curtis, "was to help get as many Citroëns on the road as I could. I wanted to start my own business, and I knew I needed a fairly large base of about 1,500 to work on, since Citroëns don't break down as often as other cars."

At about this time a friend introduced Curtis to a man who owned a lucrative $750,000-a-year motorcycle-parts business, and the man offered Curtis $300 a week to manage it. "This man," says Curtis, "didn't know how to run the business, wasn't interested in running it, and just wanted to be left alone to build motorcycle parts." Scott took the job and "all of a sudden I had to turn the company into a real business with honest books."

Curtis ran the business for a year, and even though he was putting in twelve-to-fourteen-hour days he still found time to work on Citroëns in the evenings and on weekends in order to continue building up a family of customers. Not only that, but around eleven o'clock most nights he'd jump on his motorcycle to search for a location to open a garage. A realtor finally found him a little 920-square-foot shop renting for $175 a month, and he was in business.

Curtis says he started out with $1,000 in cash and an inventory of new Citroën parts worth about $500. He also had quite an array of used parts cannibalized from thirteen to fourteen cars he had been given to tear apart, plus a half-dozen trailerloads of used parts he had picked up along the way.

Curtis launched the Curtis Circus with a base of 150 satisfied customers. He's since expanded that to more than 1,500 with a little advertising and a lot of word-of-mouth referrals, which have brought him in as much business as he, several members of his family, and three helpers can handle.

The Curtis Circus restores old Citroëns so skillfully that thirteen of his customers have already put more than one million miles on their cars. "It's a joy for me," says Curtis, "to take a Citroën that's downhill, but still has hundreds of thousands of miles left in it, and bring it back to life. I've done eight of these jobs in one year at from $8,000 to $12,000 apiece, each one with a plaque on the dash reading, THIS CAR HAS BEEN REMANUFACTURED FOR (customer's name) BY CURTIS CIRCUS (year)."

Curtis maintains a "core bank" of Citroën front-brake assemblies and other parts—produced whenever he gets a little free time—that can be instantly installed or shipped to a distant customer as needed. "We try desperately to remanufacture as many parts as possible, using present-day technology," says Curtis. As a result, many of these assemblies contain restored parts Curtis has been collecting for years.

Curtis has also developed and builds forty-seven different, easy-to-install kits, priced at from $10 to $2,000, to simplify maintenance and improve the performance of old Citroëns. "Any car maker in the world will put things where normal human beings can't get at them. The Citroën's hydraulic regulator, for instance, is located way down where the engine lives, in what looks like the Black Hole of Calcutta. Owners don't want to mess around down in that abyss, so I developed a kit that relocates this hydraulic regulator up front in the light where it can be easily maintained."

Since he first started working on Citroëns, Curtis has urged his customers to help him maintain their cars, and he has prepared illustrated step-by-step instruction sheets to help them do it. "By teaching customers how to look after their own vehicles, beginning with simple things like cleaning, waxing, changing the oil, keeping tire pressure up, and so on, you get them more enthusiastic about their cars," he says. "Pretty soon they're calling in and saying, 'Hey, Scott, it's been forty thousand miles since I changed my air filter—what should I do?' So I sell them the parts, and they supply the labor for this simple job. If I had to do it myself I'd lose my butt, since I couldn't justify charging my forty-dollar hourly rate."

Curtis's reputation has now spread to the point where he's doing business with Citroën owners throughout the United States who send him parts of their cars to be repaired (frequently accompanied by photographs of their babies lovingly named Pierre, Fifi, or something equally Gallic). One long-distance overhaul came from a Citroën owner in Chicago who started taking his transmission apart, quickly realized he didn't know what he was doing, and dumped about three hundred parts in a box that he then sent to the Curtis Circus. Curtis eventually got the tranmission reassembled and shipped it back to the customer with a bill for $1,600.

During the seventeen years since he started in business, Curtis has steadily enlarged the size of his shop from 920 to 1,500 to 2,500, and three years ago to 12,500 square feet of floor space—his latest facility boasting twenty-four car-service stalls, an office, a conference room, and, perhaps most important of all, a showroom to display an award-winning new car for which he's been named sales agent. The car is the three-wheel "Trihawk" sports car, powered by a Citroën engine, which, Curtis says, "adds a whole new clientele to the Circus" and is selling well.

The growth of his business has increased Curtis's need for money, which he's raised through a series of short- and long-term bank loans, and from private investors. Curtis had a close working relationship with a local banker, which enabled him to get four ninety-day loans of from $2,500 to $6,000 on his signature, and later, as his business grew, two long-term loans of $6,000 and $10,000. Curtis also needed money to import Citroën parts, but says his bankers didn't understand this aspect of his business ("It was like the Sunday funnies to them"), so he's gotten the cash from four private investors to whom he pays 20-percent interest a year. Since imported parts are proving to be one of the more profitable aspects of his business, Curtis feels the high interest rates he must pay for this working capital are fully justified.

The most common source of financing for new businesses appears to be personal savings, says Arnold C. Cooper, professor of management at Purdue University's Krannert Graduate School of Management. Personal savings in cash or kind have laid the foundations for some very large companies indeed. Steve Jobs sold his Volkswagen bus, and Steve Wozniak sold his Hewlett-Packard HP65 calculator, and they used $1,350 of the resulting cash to launch Apple Computer. Donald Burr went the boys one better, selling his car, home, two condominiums, and emptying his savings account to get the upfront money he needed to launch People Express.

Calvin Klein's First $10,000

Family and friends may be able to supply you with start-up money if you've got a good idea and handle them right. Brett Johnson borrowed $1,500 from his grandmother to launch the Crowd Corporation of St. Paul, Minnesota, which makes headgear festooned with ads for Coke, Skoal (snuff), Budweiser, and other products manufactured by Johnson's clients, who bought $7 million worth of merchandise from him in 1984. Fashion designer Calvin Klein started his fabulously successful women's ready-to-wear business in 1968 with $10,000 contributed by his boyhood friend Barry Schwartz, who became Klein's partner and hard-nosed business manager.*

Should you fail to get family or friends to back your new business, you might try your boss. General Electric gave two of its ex-employees $525,000 for 15 percent of their mobile-communications firm, called Mobileat Corporation located near Philadelphia. And Xerox gave five ex-managers the design for its C8/16 home computer in return for a minority interest in their new Sunrise Systems, Inc., which produces the hardware and boasts Xerox as one of its customers.

Wealthy individuals with a gambler's instinct have been known to finance intriguing ventures from Broadway musicals to glamorous restaurants with the nod often going to concepts that can be explained in a few words. One-time world karate champion Chuck Norris was in this fortunate position when he started making the rounds of Hollywood movie producers in search of $1 million to back his first film *Good Guys Wear*

*Walter McQuade, "The Bruising Businessman Behind Calvin Klein," *Fortune* (Nov. 17, 1980): 106-117.

Black. "There's four million karate people in America, " Norris is quoted as telling prospective investors. "They all know who I am. And if only half of them go to the movie that's a $6 million gross on a $1 million budget." Norris got his money, and so far the film has grossed three times $6 million.

Surprisingly enough, banks and savings institutions are excellent sources of money to start a new business provided you can meet their needs for collateral. When he was just starting out, Cabbage Patch Kids creator Xavier Roberts got a small bank loan by putting some cars up as collateral. When this money ran out, Roberts financed his young business with a Visa card, which allowed him to order up to $700 worth of fabric, thread, and stuffing per month, until he couldn't meet the payments and the card was revoked.

Herb Colvin, a young black entrepreneur, also used his car and bank money to start Suncoast Supply in a spanking-clean building a few blocks from the Tampa International Airport.

Colvin was working as a manager for Johnson & Johnson when he became fascinated by the potential of satellite- and cable-TV technology. In 1981, Colvin sold his Porsche sports car and used the cash to buy a big dish antenna, which he began experimenting with in his backyard. A few months later, Colvin incorporated Suncoast Supply to sell private television hookups, landing the Grenelefe Golf and Tennis Resort in nearby Haines City as his first customer.

Emboldened by this success, Colvin began researching the future of cable television. Within months, and with the help of the University of South Florida's Small Business Development Center, Colvin had prepared a sixty-five-page business plan for a new company to serve the cable television industry.

Colvin's data indicated that cable-television companies would soon be installing multimillion-dollar systems in major cities across the country, and that many of them, including Tampa, would insist that a substantial percentage of this business be subcontracted to minority firms.

Colvin saw this as an opportunity, so he quit his job with Johnson & Johnson and set up Suncoast Supply, which was financed primarily by a line of credit from the black-owned Community Federal Savings and Loan in Tampa, and staffed by a "rainbow coalition" of employees.

"My wife, Carole, who was working for the Hillsborough County Education Department as a speech and hearing therapist, thought I was crazy," says Colvin, but before long she left her job to become vice-president of the company, whose first customers included Cable Atlanta, Tampa Cable Television, and Times-Mirror Cable Television. Suncoast Supply did $150,000 worth of business in the first four months after it opened its doors, and in 1984 its sales totaled $1.2 million. "The days are long and tedious," says Carole Colvin, "but it's great building a business."

The next source of capital worth checking into is that provided by the federal government, which has helped thousands of people get into business—and stay there—via loans made primarily through the U.S. Small Business Administration, which has offices throughout the country.

The SBA makes or guarantees more than twenty-thousand loans a year, roughly 25 to 30 percent of them to start-up businesses. Entrepreneurs are welcome to try their luck at the SBA, where there's money available, loan conditions are somewhat less stringent than at commercial banks (two of which must reject your application before you can approach the SBA), and the paperwork required consists of a four-page form to fill out, plus a copy of your business plan.

The SBA makes direct loans of up to $150,000 at below-market rates (but only after a bank or other private lender has refused to make the loan itself), and will also issue a partial SBA guarantee to repay a loan if the borrower doesn't. The SBA will guarantee as much as 90 percent of such loans of up to $500,000 for as long as twenty-five years. The SBA also makes special loans to:

- Businesses in search of expansion money. These loans are limited to service and retail businesses grossing $2 million a year or less, wholesalers doing $9.5 million or less, and manufacturers with 1,500 or fewer employees.
- Businesses owned by low-income, economically disadvantaged entrepreneurs (maximum loan is $100,000 for fifteen years), or physically handicapped entrepreneurs (maximum loan is $500,000).
- Businesses hit by fire, flood, or other natural disasters (maximum loan is $500,000 of the company's physical damage, plus up to $500,000 to offset economic losses).

The SBA lends money to state, local, and certified development companies that promote economic growth, and makes "venture" or "risk" investments through Small Business Investment Companies (SBICs) and Minority Enterprise Small Business Investment Companies (MESBICs), which add the SBA's money to their own funds used to lend money to small businesses, buy an equity interest in them, or both. SBICs and MESBICs consider a small business to be one with assets under $9 million, net worth of less than $4 million, and average net income after taxes of under $400,000 a year.

The U.S. government also makes money available to business through the following agencies:

- The Department of Commerce's Economic Development Administration, which guarantees up to 80 percent of the face value of loans ranging from $550,000 to $10 million made by private lenders to businesses intent on using the money to create or save jobs in high unemployment areas.
- The Department of Agriculture's Farmers Home Administration, which set aside $150 million in fiscal 1985 to guarantee 90 percent of loans of up to $10 million made by commercial lenders to businesses and industries in rural areas, and up to $20 million for new fuel alcohol plants using

farm products as feedstocks. The Reagan Administration, however, completely eliminated this loan guarantee program in its fiscal 1986 budget, which was submitted to Congress early in 1985.

- The Department of Housing and Urban Development, which loans money to cities and towns, who reloan it to entrepreneurs, or put up buildings or buy equipment that can be leased to them.

Ghost Town Insurance

Quite a few municipalities around the country have been doing everything they can to encourage the starting of new businesses to replace dead or dying ones that are threatening to turn those communities into ghost towns. Duluth, Minnesota, is a perfect example.

This once-flourishing shipping center for grain and iron ore has seen mining companies close and others, like Jeno's Pizza, move away, and its unemployment rate soar to 17 percent. "There's a direct correlation between the surge of interest in small business and the unemployment situation here," the city's Executive Director of Community Enterprises told a reporter who was writing for *In Business* magazine about how "Entrepreneurial Spirit Is Saving Duluth." Duluth has set up assistance groups to help entrepreneurs obtain capital, low-rent office space, and support services from accounting to secretarial. The city has even raised several million dollars to purchase successful businesses so they can be moved to Duluth.

One local resident who moved from Duluth's unemployment rolls to running his own business is Neil Mathison, who was laid off as a corporate pilot, then lost his job as a salesman for an aircraft company. With no other job in sight, and some help from Duluth's Community Enterprises, Mathison opened North Country Aircraft Sales, specializing in buying and selling used Cessna single-engine airplanes. "It was start up or starve," says Mathison, who's building a track record, expanding his lines of credit, and looking forward to a profitable future.

Cities and states throughout the country are extending all kinds of help to entrepreneurs these days, and they'll give you the red-carpet treatment if your business is involved with high technology. The National Governors' Association in Washington, D.C., has published a booklet called *Technology & Growth: State Initiatives in Technological Innovation*, which contains a thorough rundown on what the various states have to offer, including venture capital, tax credits, customized job-training programs, entrepreneurial incubators, research parks, and industry-targeted university research.

Easily the most highly publicized source of financing for new businesses is venture capital, which got its start in the United States when the Rockefellers, Phippses, Whitneys, and other well-heeled families began looking around for new ways to preserve and expand their immense fortunes. One of the few ways to do this legally was to set up venture-capital firms like the Rockefellers' Venrock, Inc.—an early investor in Apple Computer—which sink millions into risky young companies that could quickly go bankrupt, but might conceivably multiply their money five to ten times within five years.

America's old-money families have been joined in recent years by newcomers to the venture-capital game, such as San Francisco's Arthur Rock, who made his millions by taking fliers in high-tech start-ups such as Teledyne, Intel, and Apple Computer. The latest arrivals on the venture-capital scene are giant financial corporations such as New York's Citibank, Manufacturers Hanover Trust, Prudential-Bache, and Morgan Stanley, which earlier this year announced that it had raised $40 million to "participate in new, private research and development projects with leading technology companies."

Venture magazine estimates that nearly $2 billion a year in high-risk capital is now flowing into promising new businesses, up from a paltry $39 million as recently as 1979. One reason for the quantum leap was the sharp 1978 cut on venture capital winnings, followed by a further reduction in 1981. This hyped the already surging interest in the 20-percent, 30-percent, or even 50-percent-a-year pretax returns that can be made on venture deals, and helped pull $4 billion of new money into the venture-capital industry in 1984, increasing its total resources to a new high of $16 billion, according to the *Venture Capital Journal*.

The Art of Execution

Fortunately for the cash-rich venture-capital industry, there are plenty of places for its money to go. "There are more good investment opportunities today," says venture capitalist Benjamin Rosen, "than we have the people or time to apply ourselves to—they're just unbounded. There was a key invention in the seventies that's probably behind 90 percent of all the start-ups we look at, and that's the microprocessor. Every one of our companies directly relates to the microprocessor. Speaking from ignorance, I suspect that in the biotechnology area we have the equivalent of the microprocessor. Genetic engineering is a new technique that's going to spawn a lot of things.

"We believe a business plan is a good discipline for entrepreneurs to make their dreams tangible. What it really does is tell you whether you have potentially a $1-million, $10-million, or $100-million business. It helps you organize your thoughts, not something we place a high degree of credibility on. The reason is there is no way you can actually forecast the financial future very well, and a large part of the business plan deals with the five-year forecast. For example, we backed Lotus

Development on the basis of their forecast that their first-year sales would be $3 million. They ended up doing $53 million, so we were off by a factor of seventeen. COMPAQ underestimated their first-year forecast by a factor of three, and we thought their original forecast was so wildly optimistic we really didn't believe it. Most business plans miss substantially in one direction or the other. The problem is we never know which direction. Fortunately for us, both Lotus and COMPAQ were in the right direction.

"The way we work is that we make a deal at the outset. The founders get so much stock, the financial backers so much, it's negotiated. Every company needs three and sometimes four rounds of funding before it goes public, and we are absolutely adamant that milestones be met before we do any more substantial financings. We attach a high degree of importance to our entrepreneurs meeting their milestones. They've got to know how to execute. If they can't execute on schedule, it has a disastrous impact on their future success. The ability to execute is much more important than having a proprietary product. There's very little that's proprietary today. Anything that one person can do, somebody else can do in six months. Entrepreneurship is the art of execution."

David T. Thompson, National Coordinator for Venture Financing with the big New York accounting firm of Deloitte Haskins & Sells, believes you'll have trouble attracting venture capital if your new business has

- few salable assets to liquidate if the company goes bust;
- low product-development costs, making it easy for competitors to rush into the market;
- rapidly changing technology, leading to fast product obsolescence;
- a hard-to-sell product whose advantages over the competition aren't readily apparent;

- a "revolutionary" product;
- only one product, and no others in development;
- incomplete or inexperienced management;
- an unproven or low-growth market environment.

The best way to meet a venture capitalist is through a personal introduction; if you don't know someone who can arrange it, try asking your banker or accountant for help. If all else fails, there's nothing wrong with approaching a venture-capital firm cold, either by phone or letter. The National Association of Small Business Investment Companies, 618 Washington Building, Washington, D.C. 20005, publishes an inexpensive list of more than two-hundred SBICs; Venture Economics, Inc., P.O. Box 348, Wellesley Hills, Massachusetts 02181, publishes the considerably more costly *Pratt's Guide to Venture Capital Sources*, which lists the addresses and investment criteria of more than six-hundred U.S. venture-capital firms.

Few of these firms will give your proposal a second glance if it's not accompanied by an impressive business plan built around a strong management team. "When we look at a business plan," says Jacqueline C. Morby, general partner of TA Associates in Boston, "the first page we flip to is the management section. Our ideal start-up company—one that's likely to get funded—has a team composed of: (1) a CEO with profit and loss experience gained at a major company; (2) a strong marketing person with background in product planning and management; and (3) a high calibre technical person who has developed products before and can manage a development team."

Since the venture capital community is fairly close knit, you should be careful that your proposal doesn't get a reputation of having been shopped around. "There's definitely an element of risk for the entrepreneur in deciding how many venture capitalists to show the plan to," says Bryan Cressey of Golder,

Thoma and Cressey in Chicago. "If it's only one, he might not get the best deal. If it's more than ten, the venture capitalists might not pay attention. The first thing I look for is the copy number on the plan," says Cressey. "If it's over twenty, I don't look much further. Some guys have learned that, so now they're trying to disguise the copy number. I saw one yesterday that was #CP318. It sounded more like a football play than a plan."

If you've got an unusually intriguing concept for a new business, and a crackerjack team to get it off the ground, there's a chance you can raise the start-up money you need by selling shares to the public. Securities Data Company, a New York financial information service, says that sixty-five unseasoned companies with zero to $100,000 in yearly revenues raised nearly $411 million through initial public offerings in 1984.

The key to doing a no-history financing is to find an underwriter, such as D. H. Blair in New York, Steiner Diamond in Chicago, or Robertson, Colman & Stephens in San Francisco, who may be willing to try and sell your stock to the public because of the quick killing they can make if all goes well. Underwriters are normally paid a fee in cash, along with warrants to buy shares in your company at a low price. They make their money if investors rush in and bid up the price of the offering to the point where they can sell out at a nice profit.

No book can list even a fraction of the sources of capital available to entrepreneurs, which means you may have to do some fairly heavy-duty sleuthing.

Obvious places to begin are your local bank, finance company, chamber of commerce, Rotary, office of the mayor, executive office of the governor (a staffer should be able to direct you to someone in your state's department of commerce), and your Congressional representatives in Washington, D.C.

Other potential leads worth pursuing are Small Business Institutes and Small Business Development Centers located on hundreds of university and college campuses, the Service

Corps of Retired Executives (SCORE) working out of SBA offices, volunteer organizations such as the Interracial Council for Business Opportunity, and people who advertise in *The Wall Street Journal, The New York Times,* and elsewhere as having "Capital to Invest." These ads should be read with a great deal of skepticism. Some of them appear to be misprints, for example, "Now Available, $1 million Up to $10 million for any purpose," or "SMALL BUSINESS LOANS, Min. $10,000. Fast closings. Credit not important." People looking for capital can also advertise in these publications, as dentist Philip L. Hirschorn did with a $2,000 "tombstone" financial ad in *The Wall Street Journal* that netted him $2.4 million to start a chain of combined dental and emergency medical centers.

One final bit of advice to keep in mind as you're shaking the money tree is that you don't have to grab the first financing offer that falls into your lap.

Carole Hires, Bea McHugh, and Mary Ellen Gaffney turned down two offers of seed money to start a home health-care business in Morristown, New Jersey, before they found one that appealed to them. The three women shared twenty years of nursing experience, had put together a detailed business plan, and had, in Carole Hires, a partner who had managed a firm experienced in taking care of invalids and convalescents in their homes.

Hires says two venture capitalists offered to finance the three women in exchange for 60 percent of their business. "I know the kind of work you have to put into a new venture to get it rolling," says Hires, "and felt it would be self-defeating if I accepted their offer. This was truly our last resort."

Hires then went to the Small Business Administration, which offered to loan her a lump sum of $75,000 to $100,000. Hires turned this down because she didn't need that much money to get the business started, and figured she could reduce the company's interest payments by arranging a line of credit she could draw on as needed.

Hires finally got a $130,000 line of credit from New Jersey's Horizon Bank, the partners opened their business on January 1, 1984, and in the first year they racked up billings of close to $1 million.

6

It Takes More Than Money

"It takes more than money to make a business succeed. You must also know what you are doing."

—Mary Kay Ash,
*Founder and Chairman,
Mary Kay Cosmetics*

When Suzy Bass decided to start a business of her own, she was a recently divorced lawyer's wife in Dallas, mother of two (ages four and eight), had trouble seeing without her glasses, didn't weigh much over 110 pounds soaking wet, yet started up a company delivering fifty-pound bags of ice to bars, restaurants, and other customers in Austin, Texas, whose sales are nearing $400,000 a year.

Bass had $12,000 from her divorce settlement to start a business and live on until she began making money selling ice. But as she quickly found out, launching a business takes a lot more than money. It takes contacts, production equipment, materials, vehicles, a building, employees, suppliers, know-how, perseverance, and other resources.

Suzy Bass began her search for a winning business by checking out a number of concepts, including boutiques and hobby shops, which she decided couldn't provide her and her children with a decent living. Then she bumped into an unexpected resource in the form of a friend who owned an ice company, and was reminded of a problem that had plagued a restaurant where she had worked some months earlier. It seems the restaurant's ice-making machine kept breaking down, forcing the restaurant manager to send the busboy out to a nearby convenience store to buy high-priced bags of ice cubes, when he was badly needed to clean off tables.

Bass immediately realized she had stumbled on a concept for a niche business—emergency ice service. But before spending a penny of her $12,000 to get it started, she talked with people in the ice business in Houston and San Antonio, and visited movie theaters, clubs, bars, restaurants, caterers, and other potential customers in Austin, all of which gave her enough self-confidence to set up Flash Cubes Fast Ice Delivery.

Bass was no sooner in business than trouble struck. She was turned down when she tried to lease ice-making machines and an ice-delivery truck. "They were very frank," she says. "As a woman with no credit rating, no training, and no business background, I was not a very good risk." But a friend from Houston came to her rescue and helped her get an ice machine, and another resource materialized in the shape of her old Honda hatchback, which she pressed into service as a delivery truck.

Bass's next problem was finding a home for her business. She needed a place that was cheap, centrally located, and had high ceilings and a loading dock. She eventually found one in an old warehouse. At last she was ready to rush emergency ice deliveries to potential customers she had been lining up for months. And to make sure they didn't forget her, she gave them stickers to affix to their ice machines. The stickers listed her company's name, telephone number, and business hours from 4:00 P.M. to 10:00 P.M., when she thought demand would be the greatest.

Flash Cubes' first call came at 8:00 A.M., and before Bass knew what hit her, she was working a twelve-hour day unloading tons of ice from the ice machine, putting it into bags, loading the bags in her Honda, driving to her customers' places of business, unloading the ice, handling the receipts, keeping the books, making sales calls—everything, all by herself. "It was overwhelming, exhausting, absolutely exhilarating," says Bass. "I accomplished more physically and in every other way than I would have ever imagined I could do." And as if this wasn't enough, Bass was also looking after her children, often bringing them with her to the warehouse, where she kept puzzles, games, and two cots, or dragging them along when she made her deliveries.

Bass was working virtually flat out when Flash Cubes' first growing pains began to appear. Thirty days after launching her business, she was delivering so much ice that she needed a truck to replace her old Honda hatchback. The first bank she went to for a truck loan turned her down, but a second one said yes, and she immediately gave it all her banking business. Then one night while making a delivery she broke her foot, a potential disaster because there was no one else to do the work. This forced Bass to hire her first employee, giving her time to sit back and do some long-delayed strategic planning. Bass quickly realized she had to make more sales calls, hire a bookkeeper to do the paperwork, and draw up a plan for expansion that was heavily oriented toward marketing.

Bass used every available resource she could think of to generate sales:

- She turned the sides of her trucks into traveling billboards that read FLASH CUBES, FAST ICE DELIVERY, 474-4439.
- She sent out informational mailers to every possible customer in Austin each spring, when the ice season got under way.
- She checked the list published by the chamber of commerce of upcoming special events, and then contacted the people arranging them, to submit a bid for meeting their ice needs.

- She asked beer distributors to alert her to events they were supplying, so she could go after the ice business.
- She made friends with the people who bought ice for the restaurants, bars, theaters, and other customers she served, so that if they got jobs at other locations, they'd remember Flash Cubes.

This marketing strategy succeeded in increasing Flash Cubes' sales to the point that within two years it needed larger facilities, which Bass found in a building housing Redi-Ice, a subsidiary of the company that owns the 7-Eleven chain of convenience stores. She rented just enough space for a tiny office, a loading dock, and two ice machines, and got a bonus by being next to Redi-Ice, which provided Flash Cubes with as much ice as it needed whenever its own machines couldn't fill its orders.

Bass's next growth-related problem was the discovery that one of her employees was stealing the company blind. Flash Cubes' drivers have numbered receipt books, and each customer is given a receipt when he pays for his ice, almost always in cash. One driver, however, had broken into a drawer holding unused receipt books, and taken one whose number sequence was far in advance of those currently being used. He'd give customers receipts from this book and pocket the money. Before he was found out, he had made off with between $10,000 and $20,000. This setback encouraged Bass to be a lot less trusting with her employees, to explain to them how the large amounts of cash they handled were needed to run the business and protect their jobs, and to institute much stricter financial controls.

Suzy Bass has been in business for more than five years, runs five delivery trucks, employs ten people, and in 1984 launched a second business, called Sno Delights, which sells New Orleans–style frozen desserts in thirty flavors from trailers spotted around Austin. "I probably started out with more

Sno Delights trailers than I could really manage," says Bass, "but the business is doing very well and I'm pleased with it."

Suzy Bass's experience in starting up Flash Cubes and Sno Delights mirrors that of other entrepreneurs who have successfully conceptualized new businesses and assembled the resources needed to get them going. There is no standard procedure for collecting resources, although most new enterprises seem to travel along a path that begins with money and then moves through determining the business's legal structure, giving it a name, finding a location, providing it with equipment, arranging for services and supplies, and hiring employees.

Three Ways to Do Business

One of the earliest decisions you'll have to make as a new entrepreneur is the legal one of deciding whether you want your business to be a sole proprietorship, partnership, or corporation.

If you're going to take the family lawn mower and go into the grass-cutting business, you don't have to do anything. The mere act of getting paid for looking after your neighbors' grass makes you a sole proprietor.

The advantage is that you are your own boss, and if the business turns into another General Motors, you own it all. The disadvantage is that you are all alone. You don't have any partners to help capitalize the venture, scheme and plot with you about it, help you turn it into a success, and be right there beside you during good times and bad. As a sole proprietor you are also personally liable for all debts, and if you cut off a customer's big toe while trimming his greenery, you can get sued for everything you've got.

As a sole proprietor you can do business under your own name (Mary's Lawn Service, for instance), but if you want to use an assumed name, such as Marvelous Lawn Service, you'll have to file a "doing business as" certificate with the appropriate authorities (state, county, or city). You may also need a license or permit if you're a doctor, lawyer, or other professional, if you're involved with something potentially hazardous to human health, such as disposing of toxic wastes, or if the state or locality wants to raise some revenue with you as its collection agent.

If your business earns a profit, you must report it on Schedule C of your Form 1040 personal income-tax return, and pay a self-employment tax—a Social Security tax that in 1984 amounted to 11.3 percent on the first $37,800 of net income as reported on Schedule SE, after deducting any contributions to an IRA or Keogh retirement plan. As of January 1, 1984, sole proprietors could put 15 percent of their income or $30,000— whichever is less—into a Keogh Plan. You must estimate both your business income and self-employment taxes and send any money due to the Internal Revenue Service four times a year, on forms supplied by the IRS.

If you feel you'd like to have someone share the load with you in starting up a business, you should think about a partnership. Under this arrangement, you and your partners are personally liable for the firm's debts, or for judgments if it is sued, but the responsibility for actually running the business can be divided any way the partners wish.

It's asking for trouble if you don't have a signed contract with your partners, one that spells out everything you've agreed on, from who puts how much money into the venture, to who does what, to how the profits and losses will be divided. While the partnership must file an "information return" (Form 1065) with the IRS each year, it's up to the individual partners to report any money they've made out of the business on their personal tax returns (Schedule E), and any Social Security taxes on Schedule SE.

Few relationships, including marriage, are subject to as much *Sturm und Drang* as partnerships, which are delicate organisms whose survival depends on clearly defined lines of authority, communication, and respect for your partners' management style, be it dictatorial, consensual, or something in between.

Three young Californians—two of whom were unemployed and living on food stamps—started discovering this fact of partnership life in 1974, shortly after they began developing a cheesecake recipe into San Francisco's Just Desserts bakery, whose sales in 1984 topped $5 million.

Partners Elliot Hoffman and Gail Horvath ran into trouble immediately because they were married, and their frantic business life kept complicating their private life. The solution: Gail put some distance between herself and her husband by managing the firm's store in downtown Embarcadero Center, and later by taking two years off to have a child, and then returning to the business in a new capacity.

Just Desserts was late in dividing up jobs, and the partners kept getting in each other's way. "It was a nightmare," says partner Barbara Radcliff. Elliot Hoffman took charge of business matters but kept hanging around the kitchen. "Giving up the kitchen," he says, "was like tearing my heart out." The partners were also working so hard they barely had time to talk to one another. "During that period when we weren't communicating regularly," says Radcliff, "it was not always clear what was going on. We began to lose rapport, and planning became unfocused." The partners have since worked hard to install clearer structure, job descriptions, reporting relationships, and so on, all helping to make everyone's work life at the bakery less stressful.

You can always dissolve a partnership, of course, and one way to do it is to buy out your co-venturers. Stina Hans, who with two partners founded Mini-Computer Business Applications of Montrose, California, in 1975, bought them out five years later, becoming sole owner of this fast-growing corporation whose sales reached $7.3 million in the year ending March 31, 1984.

Defusing a Time Bomb

If you're still uneasy about that unlimited-liability time bomb ticking away in a sole proprietorship or general partnership, then you should incorporate. You could try protecting yourself by purchasing a liability insurance policy to reimburse you if you are held financially responsible for your business's transgressions—but not its unpaid bills. You might even be able to get a general partnership to invite you in as a silent limited partner, which protects you against everything but losing your investment.

But the safest way to avoid being impoverished by your business going belly-up is to incorporate. This way, if things turn sour, all you lose is what you've sunk into the business. Your home, car, and other personal assets cannot be touched by your company's creditors, or by those who hold judgments against you. One way your private property can be seized is if you've agreed to be personally liable for your company's debts, something most banks will insist upon if you're just starting in business and ask for a loan.

There are other worthwhile advantages to incorporating your business. Two of the most important are (1) that the IRS will allow you to deduct the cost of medical, life, and disability insurance for your company's key people, and (2) the first $100,000 of corporate profits is taxed at an effective rate of only 26 percent, compared to the 50-percent tax you might have to pay if you took the money out of the business and declared it as personal income.

There are also drawbacks to incorporation. High on the list are these:

- It's expensive, with legal costs alone running into hundreds or thousands of dollars.
- It generates time-consuming formalities and paperwork, including stockholder meetings, keeping minutes of those meetings, sending out periodic stockholders' reports, and filing a variety of forms with various government agencies.
- Its profits are subject to corporate taxes, and any part of them paid to you and other stockholders in the form of dividends is taxed again as personal income. (This double taxation can be avoided by setting up a Subchapter S Corporation—as the Kolences did with their Palo Alto Brewery—which still limits your liability if the company goes under or is sued, but allows any profits to flow directly to you as personal income. Its big disadvantage is that you can't retain any untaxed profits in the business, as you can in a regular corporation.)

As you get closer to starting a business of your own, the fear of being isolated and lonely may begin worrying you, as it has so many others. A good way to quickly allay this fear is to join a support group of other business people in your community, such as the chamber of commerce or Rotary. Joseph Sonnenreich runs a successful unincorporated one-man advertising agency out of his apartment in New York City, and for more than twenty years he has belonged to the League of Advertising Agencies, a group of eighty or so small- to medium-size privately owned ad agencies. Sonnenreich can chat with other League members whenever he feels like it, and uses the group as a clearinghouse for locating photographers, artists, graphic designers, and other specialists he can hire as needed. "The free exchange of information saves loads of time," says Sonnenreich, "and all the members are willing to share expertise." San Francisco's Briarpatch Network was created in 1974 "to encourage like-minded people to help each other" by sharing their business knowledge and experience. And in Connecticut the first and largest of a new breed of nationwide Venture Capital Clubs was recently launched, in which entrepreneurs, attorneys, engineers, inventors, and others interested in business get together each month to hear speakers, discuss any products or services they may have to offer, and seek financing for members' new business concepts.

By now you should be far enough along in developing your own business concept to begin thinking about what to name it. Good business names are money in the bank, even though some of the best known ones are the result of pure serendipity. Steve Jobs and Steve Wozniak were thinking about calling their computer company Executek or Matrix Electronics until Jobs, a onetime fruitarian, suggested Apple. A friend of Frank and Dan Carney's mother showed them an article in the *Saturday Evening Post* about a new concoction called pizza and suggested they open a pizza restaurant in a building she owned in their hometown of Wichita, Kansas. The boys leased the building, which looked like a hut, so they named their place Pizza Hut. By the early 1970s, Pizza Hut had grown into the world's largest chain of pizza restaurants, and the brothers sold the company to PepsiCo in 1977 for $316 million.

The best names are those that tell at a glance what business you're in—Dunkin' Donuts, 5 Minute Oil Change, Just Pants, Nursefinders, and Yummy Yogurt. Superlawns is a better name than Nitro-Green for a lawn-care company, just as Kwik-Kopy has an edge over Sir Speedy in the fast-copy business.

Coming up with memorable names for companies and their products is being taken so seriously these days that it's given birth to at least one firm specializing in this business—San Francisco's NameLab, whose clients include RCA, Chrysler, Honda, and Federal Express. NameLab's best piece of work to date is "Compaq" to describe a new company that intended to sell portable computers and went on to chalk up the highest first-year sales in U.S. history. NameLab founder Ira Bachrach believes product names should be as memorable as the monikers of the companies that make the products. His nominee for one of the most effective brand names ever devised: "DieHard," to identify Sears's line of long-lasting batteries. Bachrach has even invented an index for measuring how well consumers will remember a product's brand name, using a scale from -5 to $+5$. His name-memorability ratings for three mythical packaged noodles-in-a-cup products, for example, are "Dehydrated Noodle Dinner" (-3), "Instant Mini-Meal" (0), and "Wacko Snacko" ($+5$).

Securing good working facilities and support services are critical to any start-up business, and here too there are options to match your every need.

Hothouse Entrepreneurs

One welcome development on the facilities front is something called entrepreneurial "hothouses" or "incubators," where workspace, conference rooms, canteens, part-time secretarial help, telephone-answering services, furniture rental, van rental, and the like are available on a "pay for what you use" basis. Universities including Rensselaer Polytechnic Institute in Troy, New York, and Yale University's Science Park in New Haven, Connecticut, offer more chic incubators with access to faculty consultants in business and engineering, and graduate students to provide what one wag has dubbed "slave labor."

Loren A. Schultz, an entrepreneur who's started several businesses, including Decision Data Computer Corporation, which is now a $100-million company, is building a string of incubators called Technology Centers International, headquartered in Montgomeryville, Pennsylvania, which feature business advice coordinated by a resident "Center Champion." The "Champion," who is usually a person with considerable management experience, helps companies draw up business plans, secure resources including venture capital, launch the business, and then shepherd it into the black. Schultz says he plans to have ten Centers in operation by the end of 1985, and will get his "major rewards" from investing in Center businesses that succeed.

Incubators for start-up businesses are a concept whose time has come, and in the months ahead, some fairly exotic varieties will undoubtedly be launched, such as Kitchen Privileges of Alexandria, Virginia, founded by Saul Barry Wax and partners. "We are the first business in the country," says Wax, "which was started to rent commercial kitchen space." Wax's kitchen is fully equipped, licensed by local, state, and federal health authorities, and can be used by up to six cooks for as many as fourteen hours a day at a cost of twenty-seven dollars per hour. Wax sees his kitchen as a "hothouse" for entrepreneurs turning out new food products. "They can spend $300 to produce a product," says Wax, "and if it doesn't work, they haven't lost a lot. If it succeeds, he adds, his kitchen is designed to handle their output until they need one that's entirely their own.

In its own way, the U.S. free-enterprise system is a kind of sea-to-shining-sea incubator where all the ingredients needed to turn a concept into cash can be purchased "off the shelf" as needed.

Richard Manney, founder of Mediators, Inc., a twenty-year-old media buying service in New York City, had always wanted to control his own product, and in 1982, with his associate, Tom Settineri, he used this "off-the-shelf" approach to roll out MBC Beverages. MBC's capital was largely obtained from New York's Morgan Guaranty Trust bank. Its product was a family of diet sodas formulated by Hurty-Peck & Company of Indianapolis. The soda is sold in concentrated form to bottlers who make it, package it, and sell it to food brokers who ship it to warehouses, which then distribute it to supermarkets around the country. MBC's key "off-the-shelf" ingredient, however, is the name of its new soda—"Sweet 'n Low"—obtained under an exclusive license from the Cumberland Packing Corporation of Brooklyn, New York, which makes the low-calorie sweetener.

Conserving cash is critical to any start-up business, and there are innumerable ways to do it.

One of the most common ways to conserve cash is to lease what you need, instead of buying it outright. Almost anything not consumed in your business can be leased, including structures, production machinery, office equipment, vehicles, and now full-time employees (including yourself). Employee leasing, or "contract staffing," is itself one of the nation's fastest-growing new industries, with the number of leased workers zooming from an estimated 4,000 in 1983 to 60,000 today and, according to one expert quoted by *Nation's Business*, to 10 million in the next ten years.

There are currently some two-hundred employee-leasing firms, of which Omnistaff in Dallas is the largest, with more than 7,000 employees working for 1,000 clients in fourteen states. You can pay one of these firms to take over your present staff, as well as advertising, screening, interviewing, and selecting the best candidates for whatever jobs you have to fill (or you can handle this yourself, along with discipline, promotions, and firing; this is called "unleasing"). The leasing firm's main job, however, is to prepare your weekly payroll, handle withholding taxes and Social Security payments, take care of unemployment and workers' compensation insurance, fill out W-2 forms, and generally relieve you of paperwork so you can concentrate on running your business. The cost for this service runs anywhere from 4½ to 10 percent of your payroll, plus the actual outlay for your employee-benefit program, which the leasing firm will also manage.

"Famous" Amos's Cookie Swap

Precious cash can also be saved by bartering for essential resources, as Wally "Famous" Amos did early on, when he swapped

$750 worth of his chocolate-chip cookies for advertising time on a local radio station. Another strategy is to pay for what you need with equity in your business, thus turning your suppliers into partners. Management search firms, accountants, advertising agencies, public-relations firms, management consultants, lawyers, and other providers of professional services will often reduce or eliminate their fees in return for some kind of participation in a cash-strapped new business.

Robinson, Wayne, Levin, Riccio & LaSala, a leading New Jersey law firm headquartered in Newark, did extensive legal work for a limited partnership building garden apartments in Tucson, Arizona, in return for a smaller-than-usual fee, plus a share of the partnership's profits, as well as its losses and tax credits. The firm also took stock and warrants in a new company that later went public, giving it a much larger payback on its legal services than it would have realized if it had taken its fee in cash.

Although most new businesses start out as sole proprietorships run by a single person like Suzy Bass, they cannot grow without the help of good employees, and nowhere is this better illustrated than with men and women working for high-tech companies who decide to strike out on their own, taking a handful of key people with them as co-venturers.

When James Meadlock left IBM to start Integraph, Inc., in Huntsville, Alabama, in 1969, he took with him four of his engineers and his secretary (the latter became his wife and an executive vice-president of this $400-million computer-aided design company). Meadlock started Integraph with $39,000 of his own money, and within two years after it went public in 1981, he was worth $80 million.

The point is that if you want to succeed in a business of your own, you've got to find, hire, manage, and motivate good people. You'll know you've failed if you arrive at work one day and find that one of your employees has stuck a sign up on your wall reading, "Those who believe the dead never come back to life should be around here at quitting time."

"Managing people is at least one-third of running your business," says William H. Scott, Professor of Applied Business Management at the University of New Hampshire. "Most people are satisfied and will work up to 100 percent when provided with adequate pay, a sense of security, opportunities for social interaction, and decent working conditions. To receive exceptional and enthusiastic performance," Scott adds, "you must also give the employees a sense of growth, recognition, achievement, and opportunities for participation."

Among the easiest—and most cost-effective—ways to do this is by installing an employee suggestion program, one that encourages workers to come up with ideas for saving the company money, and rewards them when they do. There are some three-thousand formal suggestion programs operating in the United States today, according to the National Association of Suggestion Systems in Chicago, and in 1984 they generated a total of 300,758 ideas, which saved employers a cumulative $800 million or so after subtracting the $98-million cost of the awards. Not a bad return on investment, and the beautiful part is that it's available to even the smallest company on the block.

In their book *The 100 Best Companies to Work for in America*, published in 1984, authors Robert Levering, Milton Moskowitz, and Michael Katz said their research has convinced them that small companies are better places to work than big ones. One reason is the imaginative ways smaller firms have for making their people feel part of the team, which the authors list as the third most important characteristic of blue-ribbon employers, after good pay and strong benefits. For example:

- Two months after joining Apple Computer, employees are loaned a computer, and ten months after that, it's theirs to keep.

- If Advanced Micro Devices chairman and founder Jerry Sanders shows up late for work at the company's Sunnyvale, California, headquarters, he has to park his Rolls-Royce in the overflow lot across the street.
- The Olga Company of Van Nuys, California, has small groups of its employees (called "associates") meet every week to tell the management of this maker of women's undergarments how they think the company could be run more efficiently.
- People Express in Newark, New Jersey, stresses "self-management," in which every employee—each of whom must own at least one-hundred shares of stock in the airline—is urged to look around the company for work they'd enjoy doing, or that needs to be done. Flight attendants may spend time on the ground doing scheduling, pilots may take a turn at marketing this cut-rate, no-frills travel service, which has turned People Express into a fast-growing money-maker in an industry famed for its red ink.
- Quad/Graphics, Inc., of Pewaukee, Wisconsin, has a once-a-year "Spring Fling and Management Sneak" in which its managers abandon this printing company for a day of meetings and a visit to the Milwaukee Art Museum, leaving the "partners"—the employees—to run the business unsupervised.
- Tandem Computers is famed throughout Silicon Valley for its Friday-afternoon "beer busts" in which everyone from the president on down assembles on the patio outside the company cafeteria for free suds and small talk.

The ultimate strategy for getting the most out of your company's human resources is to motivate them to excel, and few entrepreneurs put more energy into doing this than Mary Kay Ash, whose Dallas, Texas, cosmetics company is listed as one of the one-hundred best companies to work for in America.

Mary Kay is probably America's top woman entrepreneur, having built Mary Kay Cosmetics from a 500-square-foot Dallas storefront in 1963 to a company whose shares are traded on the New York Stock Exchange, and whose 194,000 or so independent "beauty consultants" sold some $300 million worth of skin-care products, toiletries, fragrances, and related items at "beauty shows" held in private homes across the country in 1984.

"The best reason to start a new company," says Mary Kay in her autobiography, "is that *there is a need for what you have to offer*. When we began, no cosmetic company was offering skin care. All of them were just selling rouge or lipstick or new eye colors. No company was teaching women how to care for their skin. So we came into a market where there was a real need—and we filled it."

Mary Kay says the lowest point in her life was right after World War II, when her husband, the father of her three children, came home and announced that he wanted a divorce. Suddenly Mary Kay had a family to support, and because she wanted to spend as much time as possible with her children, she took a part-time job selling Stanley Home Products at "parties" (group sales demonstrations) held in people's houses. Mary Kay averaged ten to twelve dollars in commissions on each party, which meant she had to give three a day to survive.

At one of these parties, Mary Kay noticed something very strange. There were twenty women of all ages in the room, and each one had a peaches-and-cream complexion. After the party, everyone gathered in the kitchen for coffee, and Mary Kay watched as her hostess handed everyone little jars with penciled labels. As each lady received her jar, the hostess would make a notation in a composition book. "Now let's see, you've used number three for two weeks, so use number four for seventeen days."

It turned out these women were "guinea pigs" for skin-care products that the hostess had concocted, and Mary Kay asked if she could volunteer for the treatment. The woman told Mary Kay she had an "aging skin," and gave her a shoe box filled with her products packed in reused jars, plus a direction sheet littered with bad grammar and misspelled words. Mary Kay used the products, liked them, and eventually bought the formulas from the daughter of the woman who had owned them for years, but had never figured out how to turn them into a business. Mary Kay was confident she could do it, however, and on September 13, 1963, she opened the doors of her tiny Dallas store with nine salespeople and her twenty-year-old son, Richard, as financial administrator. The store was filled with jars of her skin-care products and used office equipment in which she had invested what she thought was a fortune—$5,000.

Mary Kay's Formula for Success

Thousands of women passed Mary Kay's store every day, but few of them came to examine her unknown line of cosmetics. Mary Kay quickly realized that if she didn't do something to get her business launched it would die, and so she decided to create some excitement by selling human-hair wigs, which were a fad at the time. She filled her store window with wigs, put up "Grand Opening" signs, and hired Renee of Paris to style wigs purchased that day, and a cute little model to serve champagne to the customers.

About a dozen wigs were sold on opening day, but the next day most of them came back because the ladies' husbands thought they looked weird. "We learned," says Mary Kay, "that it's a terrible mistake to buy a wig that's noticeably different from your own hair. A wig should supplement a woman's wardrobe, and help her look good when she doesn't have time to style her hair." The wigs also made a mess in the shop, with the hair dryers and curlers all over the place, and took up so much room that there was no space left to store cosmetics. To make matters worse, it took one of Mary Kay's Beauty Consultants about eight hours to sell and fit a wig, and at that point it was decided to concentrate on skin-care and cosmetics.

Out of that decision came Mary Kay's five steps to skin-care beauty—"cleanse, stimulate, freshen, moisturize, and protect"—achieved by using her "scientifically based products for virtually every skin type." The concept worked, and the amount of cosmetics sold in the store and at "small, intimate beauty shows" began to shoot up. First-year sales hit $198,000, and by the end of the second year they had reached $800,000. "We fail forward to success," is one of Mary Kay's favorite expressions.

Mary Kay's company is run by her son Richard, leaving her free to devote all her energy to "directing and motivating the sales organization" that is the key to her success. Mary Kay Cosmetics, like Avon, Tupperware, Shaklee, and other direct-sales companies, must attract and motivate an army of part-time salespeople who are constantly leaving the business. About 80 percent of Mary Kay's beauty consultants leave and must be replaced every year, and during that year each one sells only about $3,600 worth of cosmetics, of which she keeps $1,800. Motivating these independent saleswomen to move more merchandise and recruit more new consultants is easily the most important thing in Mary Kay's workaday life.

Mary Kay's motivational philosophy is based on what she calls the "go-give" principle, which stresses giving rather than getting. Mary Kay insists that her beauty consultants never think in terms of "How much can I sell these people today?" but rather "What can I do so these women will leave here today feeling better about themselves? How can I help give them a better self-image?"

Mary Kay uses the "go-give" principle in dealing with her independent consultants, who have no territories and can sell Mary Kay products and recruit new saleswomen anywhere they like, and outnumber the company's employees 140 to one. Consultants must pay in advance for their merchandise with a bank cashier's check or money order—no personal checks allowed—which means the company doesn't have the expense of collecting bad debts, and can pass the savings back to the consultants in the form of higher commissions.

Mary Kay is constantly thinking up new rewards to give her consultants when their sales and recruiting efforts hit certain goals. When a consultant sells her first $100 worth of cosmetics at a single show, she gets a ribbon, and when she has a $200 show, she gets another one. Consultants who recruit three new saleswomen are allowed to wear a red jacket, those who recruit five get to wear an emblem on the jacket's breast pocket bearing the letters TLC for "team leader consultant," and those rounding up eight recruits get "a very striking new emblem." All TLCs get the right to wear a gold-colored bumblebee pin on their jacket for each new saleswoman they sign up.

As the beauty consultants climb up the "Ladder of Success"—itself a reward in the form of a ladder-shaped pin with diamonds on each rung for those who reach the heights of selling and recruiting—there are other motivators, the most awesome of which are handed out each year at Mary Kay's spectacular Awards Night, held at the Dallas Convention Center. More than 25,000 saleswomen attend these extravaganzas built around a theme such as "Dreams Can Come True," which featured a four-story-high castle on stage, surrounded by knights and their ladies dancing to the theme music from *Camelot*.

While dozens of famous Mary Kay pink Cadillacs are routinely given away to sales leaders, the big winner is the Director Queen of Unit Sales, who one year recently received "two fabulous diamond rings; a gold-and-diamond necklace; a natural ranch mink jacket; a brown shadow mink stroller with Labrador fox collar and cuffs; an all-expenses-paid dream holiday in Spain for the Queen and her husband; a diamond bar pin signifying her unit accomplishment; and of course, her cherished gold bumblebee pin set with nineteen diamonds."

Mary Kay, however, does not limit herself to material rewards. Psychic motivators are no less important, and Mary Kay doesn't miss a trick. Consultants are urged to write songs about the business, and prizes are awarded to winners such as "I've Got That Mary Kay Enthusiasm." A "Crow Period" precedes each sales director weekly sales meeting, when consultants are encouraged to "crow" about their past week's successes, and everyone is invited to join Mary Kay's "Five O'Clock Club" and get up at five o'clock every morning to get a head start on completing the list of the six most important things they want to accomplish that day.

Perhaps the most treasured of Mary Kay's psychic rewards, however, is reserved for the company's directors, who come to Dallas each month for training and are always invited to Mary Kay's house for tea. Once there, they make their way to Mary Kay's private bathroom, where there's a huge round sunken marble tub. They hop into the empty tub fully clothed and have their pictures taken, which forever after occupy places of honor on their walls back home. As Mary Kay says, "It takes more than money to make a new business succeed."

7

Moment of Truth

"My motto has always been 'Attack, attack, attack.' There ain't no
mercy out there."

—Glenn R. Jones,
Chairman,
Jones Intercable

Anthony Seraphin of Conshohocken, Pennsylvania, had a business concept he figured couldn't miss. It was a process for
wrapping pleasure boats in tough plastic sheeting that shrinks
drum-tight when treated with hot air, forming a protective skin
around the boat during the winter months when it's in storage.

Seraphin's "Protect-A-Boat" concept had everything. It was
cheap, fast, and easy to apply. The pleasure-boat market it was
designed to serve was big, rich, and growing. And it was patented. Yet Seraphin's product lay dead in the water for two
years because he couldn't figure out how to sell it.

At one point Seraphin wrapped a sixteen-foot boat in his
protective plastic and hauled it everywhere he went, including
the supermarket. At another point he got so desperate he used
the boat to block the entrance to marinas so their managers
would have to look at his product and hear his sales pitch.

While this was going on, Seraphin was failing on other fronts.
He held off trying to sell marina owners on the nearby New
Jersey shore until he could rent a house at cheap after-season

rates, by which time they had already completed their winter storage plans. He also insisted on wrapping each customer's boat himself, instead of designing a do-it-yourself kit that thousands of boat owners could buy and use.

Seraphin soon fell behind in paying his creditors, and was being advised to declare bankruptcy when five local investors decided to pump $123,000 into his Protect-A-Boat, Inc., in return for 38 percent of the company. This infusion of capital, plus a public relations blitz, turned the tide. Seraphin paid off his creditors, developed a do-it-yourself kit, started spending money on advertising, and during the company's fiscal year ending June 30, 1985, posted sales of some $700,000, up from $73,000 in 1983.

The greatest concept in the world is worthless if it can't be launched into the marketplace and brought to the attention of prospective customers, whose hearts and minds belong to your competitors. Mary Kay Ash learned this lesson when she failed to attract cosmetics buyers into her store in Dallas, but did get their attention once she started holding "beauty shows" in their homes.

The Car that Never Was

Businesses beyond reckoning have gone unsung because they couldn't get noticed by consumers, or deliver a viable product if they did. A little company called Holosonics, for example, got in the news by cornering about 90 percent of all the outstanding patents on a laser photography technique for making 3-D images, known as holography. Holosonics had virtually locked up this promising technology, yet it had to declare bankruptcy because it couldn't figure out what its product was, let alone how to tell the world about it. Quite a few businesses, on the other hand, have had world-class launchings only to slip into the abyss when their products failed to deliver what their advance publicity had so beguilingly promised.

In the summer of 1947, at the age of forty-three, Preston T. Tucker unveiled his new Tucker Torpedo automobile in Chicago before an audience of three thousand starstruck car dealers who had paid up to $50,000 apiece for the privilege of selling what he had heavily advertised as "The First Completely New Car in Fifty Years."

Tucker held his "world premiere" in a huge factory that had been used to make B-29 engines during World War II, and which Tucker had leased with part of the $26 million he had raised to produce this "truly modern automobile descended from racetrack champions," which he promised would make all other cars obsolete.

A hush fell over the dealers as the curtains on a hastily built stage parted to reveal a low-slung maroon car with a "Cyclops eye" headlight, planted in the middle of its nose, which turned in unison with its front wheels. Gorgeous showgirls in strapless evening gowns surrounded the car, bearing papier-mâché replicas of some of the eight-hundred parts Tucker had supposedly eliminated from his car. "The Tucker needs no clutch," cooed one. "The Tucker needs no differential," purred another. "The Tucker needs no transmission," chirped a third.

"In three months we'll build three thousand of these," Tucker announced triumphantly as he climbed into his Torpedo and rolled down a fifty-foot ramp, where the car was instantly cordoned off by plant police in case any of the dealers tried to get a closer look.

The fact of the matter was that this whole gala extravaganza was a sham, a kind of latter-day Potemkin Village thrown up by P. T. Tucker to celebrate a car that never was. The thing he guided down the ramp was a hand-assembled monster slapped together from parts of old Cords, Dodges, Oldsmobiles, and God knows what else salvaged from junkyards and used-car lots. Tucker's Torpedo was grossly overweight, its body sagged, it leaked oil and water, was unstable and tended to wobble, couldn't be started without auxiliary power from a pile of additional storage batteries, and had no reverse gear, which meant it couldn't back up.

The car was an "engineering monstrosity" said the Securities and Exchange Commission during the final months before the Tucker Corporation—having built only forty-nine cars—was finally laid to rest as thousands of dealers, stockholders, and innocent car lovers—who had paid $2.3 million in advance for seatcovers, radios, heaters, and other accessories for an automobile that would never come off an assembly line—wept.*

Launching your business into the dog-eat-dog marketplace is every entrepreneur's moment of truth, and it pays to get a jump on your competitors by doing it with as much imagination and flair as you can muster, but, unlike Tucker, you would be well advised to begin with a first-rate product or service.

If you're opening a new retail establishment, such as an auto dealership, restaurant, gift shop, or whatever, you have a whole launch armamentarium to choose from in luring customers to your place of business. "Grand Opening" signs, eye-catching bunting, free gifts, door prizes, refreshments, a two-for-one sale, even searchlights piercing the night sky. When Selma Weiser opened her first Charivari high-fashion boutique in Manhattan, she put a go-go dancer in the window to attract business. It must have worked. Today Ms. Weiser has six stores that grossed well over $10 million in 1984. "Retailing is theater," says Irwin Greenberg, president of the fast-growing Hess Department Stores chain headquartered in Allentown, Pennsylvania.

California's Tower Records has been drawing a crush of customers to the two stores it opened in Manhattan, through the simple expedient of turning them into palaces of free entertainment. It spent $2 million on its first store decorated

---

*Lester Velie, "The Fantastic Story of the TUCKER CAR," *Collier's* (June 25, 1949):13–15, 68–69, 71.

with gleaming chrome and rainbow-colored neon pulsating against rose-and-gray walls. Overhead, fifteen TV monitors preview the latest music video hits, while a disc jockey in a glass-enclosed booth pumps out jazz, rock, and classical music to various parts of the store. On weekends, big-name artists are invited to mingle with the crowds: painter Robert Rauschenberg, rock stars Hall and Oates, singer Lou Reed, pianist Vladimir Horowitz, and the casts of hit Broadway shows.

Outsmarting the Competition

Two absolutely critical ingredients in any launch strategy are advertising and publicity, whose job it is to get your business noticed and patronized.

One advertising agency that's exceptionally good at doing that is Fallon McElligott Rice, which opened its doors above Peter's Grill in downtown Minneapolis in mid-1980, and in 1983 was named "Agency of the Year" by *Advertising Age*. The agency is an outgrowth of a free-lance advertising business called Lunch Hour Ltd., which Pat Fallon and Tom McElligott had started seven years earlier when they were working for large competing agencies and wanted, in Fallon's words, to start "the preeminent creative agency in America." In the ad announcing their new agency, Fallon McElligott Rice said they believed that "imagination is one of the last remaining legal means you have to gain an unfair advantage over your competition," and that they wanted to work "for companies that would rather outsmart the competition than outspend them." Pat Fallon, president of the agency, says that it's tough to get good advertising in today's brutally competitive marketplace without spending a good deal of money—but it's not impossible.

"What you have to realize," says Fallon, "is that this year advertisers will spend over $90 billion, which will buy a little over 200,000 impressions for every man, woman, and child in America. That breaks down to about 560 times a day somebody tries to sell you something. Of the 560 ads, seventy-six are noted, not acted upon, not remembered, just noted. Of the seventy-six, twelve are remembered, but three of those are remembered negatively. And there's a growing body of knowledge which says that if people don't like your advertising personality, they'll go out of their way not to buy your product. So the attrition rate is 9 to 560, which means more than 98 percent of all advertising is absolutely wasted.

"In advertising you've got to know what you're doing. The world's changing, it's a jungle, it's like Darwinism in spades, which makes it tough on advertisers of consumer-driven products because most ads don't work, even those done by fairly competent professionals. Good advertising can also be costly. I'd say you've got to spend $500,000 a year to get somebody serious in Minneapolis, and in New York at least $1 million. If you're just starting out and don't have that kind of money to spend, then you've got to be awfully, awfully smart, or just plain lucky. One thing I'd do is start reading every marketing and advertising publication I could find. You might also ask newspaper, radio, and TV media reps if they know of any young advertising free-lancers who do low-cost campaigns.

"When my partner and I started our free-lance business we spent almost seven years doing nothing but what in most cases were brilliant campaigns for small clients with little money. We did an award-winning campaign for a one-unit haircutting operation here in Minneapolis called 7South8th for Hair. Everybody in the hairstyling business at the time was using big fashion photos, but because they couldn't afford great photographers like Richard Avedon, the ads ended up looking stupid. We couldn't afford Avedon either, so what we did was take existing photographs of well-known people and blow them up. We used a picture of Einstein with copy that read, 'A bad haircut can make anyone look dumb.' We used a shot of Shakespeare and the line 'A bad haircut is a real tragedy.' The campaign cost the client $25,000, and every time they turned it on, their sales increased 35 percent."

Although you can consider yourself blessed if you get even a mediocre advertising campaign for $25,000, good publicity can be had at bargain-basement prices, as proven by Jeff Slutsky, who, at the age of twenty-nine, has been written up in *Inc., The Wall Street Journal,* and elsewhere for his uncanny ability to grab attention for his small business clients on the cheap. One was Brickley's Firehouse, a huge disco in Fort Wayne, Indiana, which had been open for business for six months, although nobody seemed to realize it. Slutsky had invested $10,000 of borrowed money in the place and was getting a little nervous when he heard that a local radio station wanted to hold a big party for its listeners. So he went to the station manager and invited him to hold the party at Brickley's Firehouse with the nightclub supplying all the beer and wine its listeners could drink, free of charge. "The station loved the idea," says Slutsky, "and they promoted the hell out of it. Every hour on the hour they'd tell their listeners about the big party coming up at Brickley's Firehouse. All of a sudden, people were literally lined up out into the street. We spent $2,000 on booze and got maybe $30,000 worth of exposure and instant recognition. From that day on we had waiting lines." Several years later, Slutsky used some of the money he made from Brickley's Firehouse to set up the Retail Marketing Institute, which moved from Fort Wayne to Columbus, Ohio, in 1984, and specializes in helping small—and not so small—retailers stick their heads above the crowd.

Slutsky is a busy guy, and when he's out of the office, his voice on a telephone answering machine informs callers, "We've fired our receptionist and are passing the savings on to you." Another device to save his clients money, says Slutsky, is "an off-the-shelf package which sells for $189 and is designed for ma-and-pa businesses which can't afford me as their personal consultant. The package contains a Cassette Training Program, an Advanced Training Manual packed with low-cost promotional ideas from around the country, plus a copy of my book, *Streetfighting*. I spend most of my time developing promotional programs for big-name corporations which can be implemented at their locations throughout the country and works out to be very cost-effective.

"One of the easiest and cheapest techniques I use is cross-promotion, which helps two businesses at once. When I was one-third owner of the All Sports Nautilus Fitness Center in Fort Wayne, we approached the owner of the Wildwood Racquet Club in town and showed him a magazine article in which Billie Jean King, Chris Evert Lloyd, Arthur Ashe, and other tennis stars can be seen using Nautilus equipment to increase their stamina, the power of their serve, and so forth. We told the owner of the tennis club his members would greatly benefit from using Nautilus equipment, and suggested he offer them an exclusive, half-price introductory membership in our Center, with his compliments. The first thing he asked us was 'How much is this going to cost me?' 'That's the good part,' we told him, 'it won't cost you a cent, and we'll even take care of printing and mailing the offer to your one thousand members.' The whole thing cost us a little over forty dollars, and we ended up with six new memberships worth $1,800.

"Once a business gets going, we use another strategy to really get things cooking. It amounts to giving away whatever you've got practically free for one day. We did this with a five-hundred-seat Pizza Hut in Elkhart, Indiana, that put on an 'all the pizza you can eat for ninety-nine cents' special. This promotion, which the Pizza Hut co-sponsored with a local radio station, brought so many people out of the woodwork in sub-zero winter weather that traffic was backed up for miles and the state police asked us to call the whole thing off.

"Free publicity is important, but to get it you've got to do something that's newsworthy. I remember one St. Patrick's

Day we had a chain of Irish restaurants in Chicago fly in Miss Ireland for the day. We schlepped Miss Ireland from one restaurant to the other, got a lot of attention, and I think the whole thing only cost the client $4,000. If you want to do a potato thing, you bring in Miss Idaho, for corn you get Miss Iowa, and if you're into suntan lotion, it's Miss California."

John Wayne Eats Here

"I've written about a lot of other cute promotional tricks, such as the restaurant owner who decided to drum up business by putting a sign in the window announcing, 'John Wayne Will Eat Here Next Tuesday Evening.' Sure enough, John Wayne shows up, only it's an old fellow in flannel shirt and bib overalls who shared the famous actor's name. But the people who had come out to see the real John Wayne got into the spirit of the thing and had their picture taken with the guy and even asked for his autograph. These gimmicks have limited application in real life, but I write about them because that's how I generate some publicity for myself, which helped get my picture in *The Wall Street Journal*.

"My telephone started ringing at 6:30 A.M. on the morning that *Journal* story hit, and it kept ringing until 10:00 P.M. that night. I didn't even have a chance to pee, and I had to call my parents on my other phone to get them to bring me a sandwich so I'd have something to eat, and it stayed that way for a solid week. About half the people who called bought something from me, I sold about $20,000 of my $189 promotion packages, and I picked up some clients. I still receive one or two calls a week from that article, even though it came out in October 1983."

Getting your new company noticed if you're in a highly competitive business such as computers may call for the continuing help of a full-service public-relations firm like Silicon Valley's Franson & Associates, whose charges average from $100,000 to $150,000 a year plus the chance to buy some inexpensive founders' stock in your company. Paul Franson founded his firm in late 1980, and by 1984 it was one of the country's fastest-growing PR agencies with more than forty employees in Los Angeles and San Jose serving clients such as Software Publishing and Hewlett-Packard's Personal Computer Division. Franson says, "We get two or three calls a day from companies nobody's ever heard of, looking for public-relations help, and we obviously can't take them all." Those it does take, however, can expect services such as a recent trip Franson took to New York City with a computer software client to meet his contacts at *Fortune, The Wall Street Journal, PC, Computer Software News, Computer and Electronics,* and *New York,* as well as helping the client participate in a press conference called by computer hardware manufacturer Data General.

Franson believes that young companies can do a great deal to position themselves in the marketplace, and decide what to say about their business and to whom, without spending a fortune on public relations. "You can begin," says Franson, "by reading magazines such as *Business Marketing,* attending speeches or seminars given by public-relations professionals, or going into a PR shop and saying you want to talk to them about your business. If you say you want to work with them, you'll usually get quite a bit of useful information in an hour or so and it doesn't cost anything. Some PR people will allow you to hire them for a few hours or half a day of consulting, and if you don't ask them for a written report, the cost can be fairly modest. You might also get a PR firm to help you with a specific project such as launching a new product. Finally, you ought to consider adding a public-relations professional to your board of directors. You may have to sell them some inexpensive founders' stock, but you'll get good public relations and general business advice, and probably gain access to some wonderful new contacts."

In some cases a start-up company has very little left over to spend on advertising and publicity after sinking most of its capital into developing its first product. This is fairly common among high-tech companies like the two thousand or so that have suddenly sprung up to write business software for personal computers. It's tough to get noticed in this $2-billion-a-year industry unless you can spend $4 million or so on an advertising campaign for a new product that only industry leaders such as Lotus, Ashton-Tate, and Microsoft can afford. This leaves the industry's small also-rans with little choice but to peddle their products using low-cost methods such as catalogs and pitches to computer clubs. One unusually creative solution to this poverty problem was worked out by the Rabbit Software Corporation of Malvern, Pennsylvania, a company that invested more than $1 million in a program that allows microcomputers to communicate with big mainframe machines.

Rabbit knew it couldn't afford an advertising splash big enough to give its product instant name recognition, so it decided to ride along on the coattails of another company—Convergent Technologies—whose popular microcomputers are sold in quantity to a handful of other companies that resell them under their own labels. Rabbit figured these companies would be ideal prospects for its new program. Convergent Technologies liked the idea, since Rabbit's program made its products more desirable. Rabbit benefited, since marketing its program as a private-label product in harness with Convergent meant it didn't have to pay for an advertising extravaganza to launch its product, or employ an army of people to sell and service it. The danger in this strategy, which Rabbit has chosen to accept, is that Convergent Technologies will decide to develop its own line of computer programs, or that Convergent's boxes will fall out of favor with end users.

If you're just starting out in business with scanty resources, you've got to use every imaginative strategy you can think of to rise above the pack and get noticed. For example:

- Capitalize on a well-known name and face in your advertising, as Jerry Kern did when he got perennially youthful Dick Clark, fifty-five, of American Bandstand fame, to endorse a new line of seven skin-care products made by his Beverly Hills, California, company, Skin Control, Inc.
- "Piggyback" a new market blasted open by a marketing powerhouse. The Grist Mill Company of Lakeville, Minnesota, did this when it brought out its own granola bar after General Mills had spent megabucks getting this new product on the nation's supermarket shelves.
- Butter up the salespeople responsible for getting your product into the hands of consumers. The author of a book on the stock market, who wanted to make sure it didn't get lost among all the other titles that his publisher was hawking, gave each member of the sales force one two-dollar share of stock in a new Chicago-based hotel chain, accompanied by a personal letter extolling the virtues of his book.

Manicure in the Clouds

Every product consists of benefits at a price, and both must be right if you expect your new business to succeed. Casino barons Clifford and Stuart Perlman found this out after starting up Regent Air, which offered to waft passengers from Newark to Los Angeles in Arabian Nights luxury, with prices to match. Regent Air's Boeing 727s, which were originally configured to hold 125 passengers, were redesigned to accommodate thirty-five in overstuffed leather armchairs. Passengers could get acquainted at a standup art deco bar, sip vintage wines and champagnes, feast on a sumptuous buffet of delicacies including lobster tails and caviar, and enjoy the services of a sommelier, manicurist, and stenographer—all for a one-way fare of $1,650, or about double what competing airlines were charging. Customers stayed away from Regent Air in droves, forcing the Perlmans to sell the airline. But hopes spring eternal, and Regent Air is now flying under new ownership that's cut the price of Regent's high-class accommodations to $785, which equals the price of a premium first-class coast-to-coast ticket on other airlines.

Regent Air has had trouble getting off the ground because it has charged too much for its product. But start-up companies can also come to grief by charging too little, which was the fate of Dial Dictation, a kind of precursor of today's multibillion-dollar word processing industry.

A Dial Dictation customer in New York City's financial district could pick up the telephone on his office desk, dial a special number, and have his dictation automatically recorded on plastic discs in Dial Dictation's headquarters a few blocks away. A Dial Dictation typist would then put the disc on her playback machine, insert a piece of the customer's stationery in her typewriter, and type up his letter. Dictation would be hand-delivered to the customer's office as typewritten correspondence within several hours after it was received, and before long the little company had a blue-ribbon roster of cash-rich clients, including AT&T and IBM.

Dial Dictation's trouble was that it was underpricing its product. It was losing money on every letter it typed, putting this pipsqueak firm in the ridiculous position of subsidizing corporate giants. Yet it hung on for dear life, refusing to raise its prices because it didn't want to risk losing the very business that, in a few short months, sent it gurgling down the drain.

Some pricing strategies are definitely better than others during various stages of a company's life cycle, and the Big Eight accounting firm of Price Waterhouse believes nine different ones are worth considering:

Cost-Plus Pricing: adding a set percentage to the cost of your product in order to earn what you consider to be an appropriate profit.

Skimming: maximizing short-run profits by targeting customers who place a high value on a product you've just introduced and are willing to pay a high price to get it.

Low-Ball Pricing: "buying" business by offering to sell your product below full cost in the hope of getting profitable follow-up orders in the future.

Penetration Pricing: using a low price to seize a large "untapped" share of a market in the expectation that the resulting volume will drive down unit costs and drive up profits.

Opportunistic Pricing: raising prices sharply during periods of severe shortage, at the risk of losing customers who badly need your product and will pay a higher price for it, but may get even by deserting you when things return to normal.

Loss-Leader Pricing: cutting the price of selected products in order to attract customers to take a look at your entire line.

Defensive Pricing: This is useful in protecting old products or market share by holding prices low to discourage competition, or keeping them high when pricing a new product so it won't "steal" sales from similar, already established products in your line.

Milking: a short-run profit strategy useful, for example, if you plan to gradually leave a market and are willing to sacrifice market share by maintaining uncompetitive prices with high margins.

Foul-Weather Pricing: trimming prices to stay at a level that will cover your out-of-pocket costs and make some contribution to overhead, in order to get through a recession or other difficult economic period.

Price Waterhouse notes that businesses are sometimes said to go through a life cycle consisting of Start-Up, Growth, Maturity, and Decline, and that its nine pricing strategies are often associated with these different stages as follows:

Start-Up: Skimming.
Growth: Low-Ball, Penetration.
Maturity: Loss-Leader, Defensive, Milking.
Decline: Milking, Foul-Weather.

The "Free Goldfish" Strategy

No discussion of pricing would be complete without mentioning the wildest strategy of all—giving your product away to customers free of charge. Like the pet shop that gives a free goldfish to anyone who wants one, and then waits patiently for the customer to return with five bucks to buy the fish bowl, gravel, and food (which will keep him coming back to the store for the life of the fish).

While good products sensibly priced are essential to launching a business, you'll also have to deliver quality and service if you want your business to grow. An apostle of this philosophy is "Herkie" Herkimer, the nation's number-one teacher and outfitter of cheerleaders, drill teams, and pep clubs. "Our prices are as low as possible," says Herkimer. "A student can go to one of my clinics for four or five days for under $100 and receive room, meals, and all of the training taught by the country's most talented instructors. We also manufacture the highest-quality uniforms because we realize they are worn more than any other item of clothing a girl has in her wardrobe during the cheerleading season. So we make them with good fabrics and good yarn. We also stress service. We work very hard to make our deliveries on schedule so schools can get them on time for their ball games. Any adjustments that need to be made are made cheerfully. The customer is always right, regardless. We treat our customers like kings, and they keep coming back to us."

Getting your product a beachhead in the marketplace is the single biggest challenge you'll face during the launch phase of your business. Some entrepreneurs, like Preston Tucker, never succeed in doing this because they don't have a viable product. Others not only put together a hot product, but are able to push it through one channel of distribution after another until it can be purchased throughout the U.S.A. I recently met two entrepreneurs who vividly represent both of these extremes.

The first was Marie-Claire Wadden, a trim, middle-aged artist from Canada who's literally "dreamed up" a new way of painting landscape and abstractions that has to be seen to be believed. Her concept, however, has gone nowhere in more than fifteen years.

The other is Lawless Barrientos, a young CPA from Tallahassee, Florida, who's created a new business guide that's gone from one success to another.

Wadden arrived at my door with a collection of colorful, postcard-size landscapes, each painted with what appeared to be hundreds of delicate brushstrokes that it had obviously taken an artist countless hours to complete. The landscapes contained dreamlike old barns and windmills, rainbows, sailboats, seagulls, cat-o'-nine-tails—each one a unique work of art suitable for framing.

Then Wadden showed me how her magical paintings were done. Out of an oversized handbag came a food-warming tray she had bought at a flea market for three dollars, followed by a small traveling iron, a plastic bag filled with broken crayons, and a stack of plain white postcards.

Wadden plugged in the food-warming tray, and when it was hot she placed stubs of blue and yellow crayons on it, which promptly melted, forming pools of color. She then picked up a white card and slathered it across the melted crayons, instantly creating a field of waving yellow grain against a cloud-filled blue sky.

She next plugged in her small traveling iron and melted some snippets of red and orange crayons on the warming tray. She then dipped the hot tip of the traveling iron into the droplets of melted crayons and, with a few flourishes of the iron, composed a beautiful, almost radiant butterfly in the foreground of the picture. Wadden had created a lovely miniature painting before my eyes—and it took her just over sixty seconds. On a good day, she'll turn out three hundred of these handcrafted paintings, which she then attempts to sell as greeting cards for $1.50 apiece.

Wadden and her husband, Mark, who serves as her business manager, are absolutely convinced that if her melted-crayon painting technique could be packaged as a kit, it would sell extremely well. So far, however, they've been unable to interest any manufacturer in the idea, including Binney and Smith, the manufacturers of Crayola crayons, recently acquired by Hallmark Cards, which the Waddens figured would jump at the chance to expand the market for their crayons beyond eleven-year-olds to adult hobbyists.

Lawless Barrientos's story is completely different. He created a product, and within months he had identified nearly a dozen different ways to sell it successfully.

The product is a series of *Fortune*-size booklets containing copies of all the state and federal forms, plus related information, that an entrepreneur needs to start in business in each one of the fifty states and the District of Columbia. The booklets are titled the (Name of State or D.C.) *Business Kit for Starting and Existing Businesses,* and within one year after he began working on them, he sold his five-person accounting firm at a profit so he could devote full time to publishing.

Barrientos's first kit contained the facts and forms needed to get into business in his home state of Florida, and his first sales effort consisted of having his secretary send letters offering the kit for $9.95 to every name appearing on a list, printed weekly in the *Tallahassee Democrat,* of people applying for occupational licenses.

But there were only a handful of names on the list, and so kit sales languished until Barrientos discovered a group of specialized newspapers listing nothing but the kinds of leads he needed. So he subscribed to several of them, and before long his direct-mail letters—which his secretary was still typing furiously—were pulling a phenomenal 8-percent response. The cost of getting out all these letters was proving far too burdensome, however, and so Barrientos again started looking for something better, and found it in stationery stores.

He started selling his kits through these outlets on a consignment basis, and almost immediately they started moving off the shelf at the rate of five or ten a month. "I knew I had something," Barrientos says, "because my kits were outselling Norman Dacey's *How to Avoid Probate* by two or three to one." On the strength of this success, he decided to tie in with a sales representative in Atlanta, who started marketing the kits throughout the Southeast.

Then Barrientos got another marketing brainstorm. He was going to the post office one morning, which happened to be directly across the street from the Florida Chamber of Commerce. It suddenly dawned on him that the Chamber had "a problem relating to small business people," and might like to get involved with his kit, which was designed specifically for fledgling entrepreneurs.

Unexpected Goodies

The Florida Chamber not only liked the kit, but agreed to buy them in quantity for sale through their local chambers of commerce. Barrientos sold them for six dollars apiece to the Florida Chamber, which resold them to its locals for ten dollars, and the locals sold them to their members for fifteen dollars. The Florida Chamber also agreed to be Barrientos's agent for sales to Chambers in all fifty states, and quickly got its first order for 10,000 kits from its sister Chamber in California. You'd think that by this time Barrientos would have figured his marketing system was in place. Not so.

Next came some unexpected goodies, what Barrientos calls "crossover sales."

A major bank bought one thousand kits (with an ad for its services on the cover), which it gave away to small businesses opening new accounts. The bank also had an ulterior motive. Many small-business people don't register with the state and federal government in order to avoid paying taxes. If they're caught, however, they must pay these accrued back taxes, even if at the expense of missing payments on loans they've gotten from the bank. So the complimentary kits make it easy for the bank's new business customers to register, pay the taxes they owe, and stay current with the bank.

Barrientos discovered that a similar situation exists with lawyers. They do the legal work required to get people in business, and then tell their clients to see an accountant about the necessary government reporting forms. The clients frequently delay or forget to do this, however, and when they're hit with a tax penalty, whom do they blame? Right, their lawyer. A complimentary starting business kit gets the lawyer off the hook for fifteen dollars, which is then added to the client's bill.

Barrientos is also selling his kits to franchisers (who give them to their new franchisees), as well as to states, so that they can compare their forms with other states—a useful exercise. One example: every state has an unemployment-compensation tax, and most forms ask for current and historic information, say, for three years back. Smart states don't date these three years, e.g., 1984, 1983, and 1982, but other states, like Illinois and Pennsylvania, do—which means they must reprint these forms every year at great expense. Barrientos says, by the way, that the last time he looked, New Mexico and Oregon had the best business reporting forms, and Ohio unquestionably the worst.

Not long after Barrientos started bringing out his kits, he was approached by the big New York publishing firm of Simon and Schuster, which wanted to take over the business and offered him an attractive deal. The company told Barrientos it would reimburse him for whatever he had spent setting his first kits in type, pay him for any kits he had in inventory, give him a six-figure advance against future royalties for finishing the series, and pay him a royalty on every kit sold. Barrientos took Simon and Schuster's offer, finished all fifty-one kits, and then accepted a new job as a consulting CPA with the regional accounting firm of May Zima & Company in Atlanta.

When comparing Barrientos's starting business kits with Wadden's melted-crayon paintings, several things immediately stand out.

Barrientos was far more successful in thinking like an entrepreneur. He saw the Florida Chamber of Commerce's headquarters building and said, "Hey, I think those people have a need I can fill."

His CPA training obviously helped him, as illustrated by the way he uncovered marketing opportunities and arrived at his pricing. He experimented with a variety of prices, and discovered he could sell more kits at twenty-five dollars than at five dollars. But an old farmer client had once told him that "pigs get fat, but hogs get slaughtered," so he settled on a price of fifteen dollars, which worked very well.

Finally, and in some ways most important, Barrientos already had the end product he wanted to sell, the marketing channels for putting it into customers' hands were in place and operating smoothly, and his kits were completely compatible with the product line of the company that eventually bought him out. Wadden doesn't have the product she dreams of, but only a painting technique that might be packaged into a product for hobbyists.

There are, as Barrientos discovered, innumerable consumer groups to target when marketing your product, and failure to choose the right ones can cost both time and money.

This happened to San Antonio's Primefax, Inc., which developed a computerized data base that enabled shops that repaired television and video cassette recorders to quickly match a broken set's symptoms with the most probable cause of the trouble. Primefax's data base consisted of an incredible 750,000 actual case histories of TV and VCR breakdowns, and by feeding a few key symptoms into the system, a technician could get an instant display of the half-dozen or so most likely reasons for the trouble.

Primefax had its pricing right, charging repair shops $100 for initial hookup, twenty dollars a month in connect charges to its data base, forty dollars to rent a display terminal, and five dollars for each inquiry. Primefax also launched its new business successfully, and within several months it had four hundred mainly small and independent repair shops linked to its data base. The trouble was that the repair shops' technicians saw the Primefax system as an affront to their professional competence, and refused to use it until they had tried every other trick in the book. Since the heart of Primefax's business was the income generated by technicians' inquiries, it soon realized that it was selling to the wrong group of customers.

Primefax redirected the bulk of its selling efforts toward large corporations such as Montgomery Ward, RCA, and General Electric, which had nationwide TV and VCR repair networks, and technicians who were quite willing to use its service. As a result of this strategy, Primefax now believes its troubles are over. "The foundation required for profitable growth," says Primefax's president, Royal Elmore, "is nearly completed."

Primefax could not reach launch velocity with its TV and VCR repair service until it targeted the right group of customers. Equally important is targeting your product toward the consumer need it's actually filling, rather than the one *you think* it's filling. One of the best illustrations of this on record is Kimberly-Clark's experience with Kleenex.

The first Kleenex tissues were made out of very thin and soft paper, which Kimberly-Clark of Neenah, Wisconsin, had developed for use in gas masks during World War I. The company began marketing the product in 1924 as disposable tissues to replace the usually soggy and dirty towels that women kept in the bathroom to remove cold cream from their faces at night. Kleenex was packaged in its familiar pop-up box, and the future looked bright, yet sales languished until 1930, when the company did a market survey indicating that most Kleenex customers used the tissues to blow their noses rather than remove cold cream from their faces.

Kimberly-Clark immediately began repositioning Kleenex as a substitute for cloth handkerchiefs, using one of the most famous advertising slogans of all time—"Don't Put a Cold in Your Pocket." In 1931, Kleenex sales more than doubled, allowing the company to turn its attention to a product called Kotex, which was proving even tougher to launch than Kleenex. Kimberly-Clark finally got Kotex into women's shopping bags by putting it on store counters wrapped in plain paper, so they could pick it up without asking for it. The sales success of Kleenex and Kotex helped keep Kimberly-Clark's factories humming all through the grim thirties as Victrolas blared, "Brother, Can You Spare a Dime?"*

"Absolutely Positively Overnight"

Few companies born in the half-century since the Great Depression have brought more pure joy to the investors who backed them than Fred Smith's Federal Express Corporation, which hit $1 billion a year in sales just ten years after it was launched.

Smith is the son of a millionaire bus company and restaurant chain owner who died when he was four years old, leaving him an inheritance of over $4 million.

Young Smith got his pilot's license at age fifteen, and with

---

*Sidney Furst and Milton Sherman, eds., *Business Decisions That Changed Our Lives* (New York: Random House, 1964), 151–163.

two of his tenth-grade classmates he also started up a recording studio in a garage in Memphis, Tennessee, which they called the Ardent Record Company. The boys' little business recorded local rock-'n'-roll groups performing numbers such as "Big Satin Mama," and it's still going strong today, although Smith left it at age eighteen to study political science and economics at Yale University.

While at Yale, Smith's interests in flying and business coalesced into an economics term paper describing his concept for a new industry, which nine years later he incorporated as Federal Express. Smith's term paper, on which he reportedly received a "C," spelled out his conviction that the air-freight business could never become cost-effective, hence profitable, until it was divorced from the airlines, which ran it as a rather tiresome appendage to their passenger business. To begin with, said Smith, air freight was a nighttime business, with packages ready for pickup at the end of the working day. Passenger service, on the other hand, was a daytime business specializing in getting people to their destinations before the sun went down. To make money carrying air freight, Smith continued, one needed special cargo planes, package-handling equipment, and a depot built to receive and reroute shipments quickly, so they'd arrive at their destinations early the next day. Passenger airlines were simply not equipped to do this, Smith concluded, because their planes, baggage-handling equipment, and terminals were designed for people, not for packages. The air-freight business was so marginal to the big airlines, as a matter of fact, that they tried to avoid hauling small packages of ten pounds or less, which Smith believed held the secret to making money in air freight.

After graduating from Yale in 1966, Smith entered the Marine Corps and served in Vietnam as a much-decorated company commander and later a pilot. Within weeks after his discharge from the service in 1969 at age twenty-five, Smith used his multimillion-dollar inheritance to buy a controlling interest in a money-losing Little Rock company called Arkansas Aviation Sales. Smith lost no time changing Arkansas Aviation into an aggressive and profitable buyer and seller of corporate jets.

As this business grew, Smith continued to research the possibility of revolutionizing the air-freight business along the lines spelled out in his Yale term paper. Smith visualized a system where vans driven by people dressed to look like pilots would pick up packages shortly after 5:00 P.M., and rush them to the nearest major airport, where they would be loaded onto planes and flown to a hub city. Within minutes after they arrived, they would be sorted by young college students, tossed onto fast-moving conveyor belts, reloaded on planes headed for their destination cities, and delivered before noon the next day.

Smith was determined to provide this service, and named his company Federal Express because he thought his first customer would be the United States Federal Reserve System, which he hoped would hire him to haul canceled checks between its nationwide system of member banks. The government didn't buy Smith's idea, but he kept the name Federal anyway, because he thought it had an impressive ring to it, and would attract favorable public attention to his fledgling enterprise.

Smith decided to launch Federal Express on the night of March 12, 1973. By that time he had built up an eleven-city network of pickup and delivery points, had a few little Falcon jets to carry the small packages of ten pounds or less that were to become his specialty, and was ready to push the button. On hand at Federal Express's hub city of Memphis, Tennessee, to watch the festivities, were company employees and their families, a representative of a New York investment-banking firm, and the curious. All eyes scanned the skies, waiting for the first Falcons to come in. Finally these little birds started landing. their cargo doors were flung open, and nestled inside were a total of just six packages, one of which was a birthday present from Smith to a company employee.

"We realized then that we didn't have enough cities, and people hadn't heard of us," said Mike Fitzgerald, who headed Federal's field sales force. "This introduction was a bust." So Fitzgerald and a few colleagues locked themselves in a room and rebuilt the network from an eleven- to a twenty-five-city system, and a month later, on April 17, they launched Federal Express again. This time the Falcons flew into Memphis with 186 packages aboard, and the following day Fitzgerald circulated to all of his employees a memo proudly announcing, "We are launched."*

Since that historic night, Federal Express has grown to the point where its approximately 30,000 employees and 10,000 radio-dispatched vans make as many as 450,000 pickups and deliveries every weekday to customers in 40,000 communities throughout the United States. Much of this incredible expansion has been achieved with the help of two new products: Overnight Letters and Courier-Pak Overnight Envelopes, which were joined by ZapMail in 1984. Federal Express is currently sweating out its hugely expensive, yet-to-be-proven electronic ZapMail system, which uses satellites to transmit documents between any two communities in the United States within two hours after they have been picked up at the point of transmission.

Starting up ZapMail service had put an $83-million drain on Federal Express's earnings as of the beginning of 1985 (with break-even several years away), much to the delight of John C. Emery, Jr., chairman of Emery Air Freight Corporation, one of Federal's arch rivals. In a recent interview with the editor of *Planning Review*, the journal of the North American Society for Corporate Planning, Emery said, "Today for

---

*The best book on the tumultuous launching of Federal Express is Robert A. Sigafoo's *Absolutely Positively Overnight!* (Memphis: St. Luke's Press, 1983).

the first time I saw a sample of the new Federal Express ZapMail. It's really crummy. I'm surprised that they point with such pride to a reproduction that looks like it was made on a busted Xerox machine."

One reason why Emery may be zapping ZapMail is that Fred Smith is moving Federal Express into two very profitable businesses where Emery is currently the undisputed leader— shipments of heavy cargo and the international forwarding of documents, packages, and parcels. These are large markets with great upside potential, and it's not surprising that the son of the founder of Emery Air Freight should be a little upset to have the likes of Fred Smith going after a piece of his long-term growth.

Growth, however, is what business is all about, hitting on a winning concept like Fred Smith's "Absolutely Positively Overnight" delivery of small packages and then making it happen, learning from your inevitable mistakes, introducing new products, and going head-to-head with your competitors, who would like nothing better than to eat your lunch. "Bring on the competitors, just don't block my driveway," says Ray Danner, chairman of Shoney's, Inc. (a hugely profitable $477-million restaurant chain based in Nashville whose sizzling growth record is the envy of its industry).

8

Climbing the Learning Curve

"What it really takes to create a successful new product is a thorough understanding of consumers' wishes, wants, and desires."

—William J. McDonald,
New Products Marketing Director,
Frito-Lay

As with everything else in business, there's no magic formula for growth. If there were, there'd be a General Motors on every streetcorner.

Occasionally, growth seems to materialize suddenly out of the blue, as it did for tiny Advanced Input Devices, Inc., of Coeur d'Alene, Idaho, whose sales quadrupled from $4 million to $16 million in a single year after IBM selected it to produce the keyboard for its IBM PC*jr* personal computer.

But even here, growth just doesn't happen. It comes from developing good products and selling those products aggressively. And as soon as your original products begin to take hold in the marketplace, you must begin ensuring your company's future by improving your old wares and introducing new ones. "If you become complacent in this business, you're dead," says Steve Blank, a Silicon Valley marketing executive. "It's the next product and the next and the next that keep you alive."

You don't, by the way, have to be an M.B.A. from Harvard,

Wharton, or Stanford to create a line of winning products. You don't even have to be American born and bred, speak good English, or have money in the bank. When Elie Tahari arrived in New York from Israel thirteen years ago, he had sixty dollars in his pocket and spent his first two weeks sleeping in Central Park. Today, thanks to good products expertly marketed, Tahari has a women's sportswear business grossing $50 million a year, which allows him to live in a spectacular triplex penthouse whose master bedroom overlooks his old leafy pad in the Park.

The underlying essentials for climbing the learning curve to long-term growth are the passion to build a substantial business, the ability to hire and manage good people, the determination to keep sweating the details of production and marketing, and, of course, a product that lends itself to growth (postcards painted by solitary artists won't do). "Our people want opportunity; without growth, they'd be gone," says People Express founder and chairman Donald Burr. "It's where you get your excitement and your learning; it makes for commitment and high levels of energy."

One young entrepreneur with all these attributes is Chris Nguyen, who came to the United States from South Vietnam at age eighteen, knew nothing about business, had no capital, and spoke halting English, yet has built a company that grossed $4 million in 1984, selling handmade Oriental eggrolls.

Nguyen is typical of the immigrants pouring into this country who are amazed by the opportunities here, are going into business by the thousands, and are adding a new burst of entrepreneurial vigor to the American free-enterprise system.

Nguyen left Saigon in 1966 to study chemical engineering at Trinity University in San Antonio, Texas, but switched to marketing before graduating in 1970. He then began pursuing an M.B.A. at the University of Iowa in Iowa City, but quickly became bored and quit in 1971 to start his own business.

Impostor Eggrolls

Nguyen had no trouble deciding what he wanted to do, because soon after landing on U.S. soil he became outraged by what was being foisted on Americans as Oriental eggrolls. "We made real eggrolls at home in Saigon, using an old family recipe," says Nguyen. "They were filled with meat and other good things, and they were genuine rolls made by hand instead of those pillow-shaped, vegetable-stuffed impostors manufactured by Chun King and La Choy."

Nguyen was also attracted to the handmade eggroll business because it was labor-intensive, required no expensive machinery, was an easy market to enter, and needed relatively little up-front money, which was a good thing since he didn't have any. What he did have, however, was a comprehensive business plan including three-year sales and profit projections, and two members of his immediate family—his brother Tuan and his sister Isabelle—studying at the University of Nebraska, only forty-five minutes away in Omaha.

Over the next year, Tuan and Isabelle rounded up a dozen investors including doctors, professors, an investment banker, and a farmer who agreed to put up $20,000 in exchange for close to half of Nguyen's company, incorporated as Oriental Food Delicacies, Inc. Once this $20,000 of seed money was in hand, Nguyen applied to the U.S. Small Business Administration for a $40,000 loan. The SBA told Nguyen it couldn't advance him a dime until his loan application had been turned down by three commercial banks. Nguyen quickly collected the required rejections and the SBA lent him the $40,000.

Nguyen started making sample eggrolls in a small commercial kitchen in Omaha, rented from a man who used it during the week to make sandwiches for vending machines, but didn't need it on the weekends. Shortly thereafter, Nguyen found a 1,500-square-foot kitchen approved by the U.S. Department of Agriculture for making meat products for sale across state lines. He bought some equipment and hired several people, including his sister Isabelle, who agreed to manage the production side of the business, while Nguyen took to the road with samples of what he called his "CHA-ZAH!" meat eggrolls that "were served to the royal families in the Orient" and are now "available in the West from our USDA-approved kitchen."

Nguyen started out by calling on hotels, motels, restaurants, and country clubs in Omaha. Quite a few liked his product, but gave him orders for only a few cases (seventy-two eggrolls to the case). His first break came from Omaha's Hinky-Dinky Stores, which purchased more than fifty cases after he had given shoppers at its newest store piping-hot samples of his eggrolls.

Oriental Food Delicacies posted sales of $128,000 in 1972, which was below Nguyen's projections. "The market did not take off as fast as we thought it would," he says, "because Americans were used to a bogus, contraband, misnomered item—the pillow-shaped eggroll. And when our authentic eggroll came along, few people cared for it. We got a lot of negatives."

There were other negatives, and among them was the fact that Nguyen lacked both the know-how and capital needed to buy automated eggroll-making machinery, and had to settle for whatever he could lay his hands on, including a piece of equipment originally designed for frying doughnuts.

A second negative was presented by the overly expensive ingredients Nguyen used in his first eggroll recipe, particularly imported black mushrooms, and Mexican sweet potatoes called *jicama*, which are eaten raw, like water chestnuts. Although Nguyen would eventually install the latest in cost-cutting machinery, he was able to immediately eliminate those exotic mushrooms and potatoes, which allowed him to reduce his prices. One ingredient he did not eliminate was meat, which he advertised as the very soul of his eggrolls, compared with

Chun King and La Choy, in which meat is an also-ran, and Matlow (another competitor), in which it is nonexistent.

A final negative factor was Oriental Food Delicacies' falling cash reserves, which forced Nguyen to ask the SBA for an extension on his old loan, and to guarantee a new $20,000 commercial bank loan, which it did.

"During the first few years small entrepreneurs are in business," says Nguyen, "they can get hurt by two things: undercapitalization and negative cash flow. If you've got a good capital position, you may be able to take care of negative cash flow until your business picks up. But if you are undercapitalized and get hit with negative cash flow, you can get killed."

Nguyen's initial strategy was to sell his eggrolls in the deli departments of supermarkets in the Midwest. This meant flying from city to city loaded down with samples of his product and a briefcase containing a tiny fryer and a bottle of cooking oil, so he could prepare hot and crispy samples of CHA-ZAH! eggrolls in the hallway outside prospective buyers' offices.

Oriental Food Delicacies was turning out one hundred cases of eggrolls a week in 1974, when Nguyen walked into the office of Steve Osder, Director of the Appetizer Department of Farmer Jack Supermarkets in Detroit. Osder bit into a CHA-ZAH! and liked it so much he gave Nguyen an order for six hundred cases (43,200 eggrolls). "I was so excited," says Nguyen, "that I told this fine gentleman, 'My goodness, I'm not sure I can get you six hundred cases right away. Would it be all right if I split-shipped you one hundred cases next week, three hundred cases the following week, and the rest after that?' " Osder agreed, Nguyen hired more workers, put everybody on overtime, and filled Farmer Jack's order with enough left over to keep his other customers happy.

Oriental Food Delicacies started making money in 1974, and in 1975 it passed the $500,000 mark in sales. In 1978, Nguyen moved the company from Omaha to Tampa, Florida, where he was able to rent a 9,000-square-foot, USDA-approved production facility six times larger than the one he had left behind. The future looked great. Oriental Food Delicacies' sales were growing at a healthy 15 percent a year, and Nguyen had even been able to buy back most of the shares in his company that he had sold to Nebraskans who didn't relish the idea of being 1,500 miles away from their investment. Still, there was a problem.

"The problem," says Nguyen, "was that we had a no-name product. People may have been served our eggrolls at a hotel banquet and loved them, or bought them out of a supermarket deli case and loved them, but they had no way of knowing they were ours. We had no brand loyalty. And if a buyer for a supermarket, hotel, or restaurant could purchase somebody else's eggrolls for a few pennies cheaper, he'd do so without hesitation."

To solve this problem, Nguyen decided to package his CHA-ZAH! eggrolls so customers could buy them in the frozen-food section of their local supermarket. Nguyen's CHA-ZAH! trademark appears on the package in big letters no less than ten times. And to make doubly certain that nobody ever forgets his product, he has embellished the box with a full-color photograph of a strikingly beautiful Vietnamese woman named Lo-An, who had escaped from Saigon a few days before it fell to the Communists, and whom Nguyen married shortly after arriving in Tampa.

By the end of 1982, the year in which Nguyen became a U.S. citizen, Oriental Food Delicacies had three-dozen employees turning out $2 million worth of eggrolls a year. The eggrolls were sold through a network of nearly sixty brokers and distributors serviced by one full-time salesman soon to be joined by a second. This meant that for the first time since he started the business, Nguyen could devote serious time to planning its long-term growth.

Nguyen knew his product was virtually unknown in the $100-million eggroll industry, and that he had to get his eggrolls noticed—and remembered—if he was to reach his goal of more than doubling the company's sales to $10 million by 1990. The strategy Nguyen eventually hit upon to accomplish this had three elements: gifts, humor, and the beautiful Lo-An.

Nguyen's first move was to start doing business as Lo-An Delicacies, which allowed him to make even greater use of his wife as the company's fetching image. Lo-An's name and face soon adorned all the company's packaging, its stationery, its "Lo-Angrams" ("Important Message from Lo-An Delicacies"), and even highway billboards, which have Lo-An posing the question, "Haven't you had my eggrolls lately?"

The Phantom Yacht Club

Nguyen next began stocking up on gifts of every description to be given to his brokers: coffee mugs, T-shirts, polo shirts, lightweight jogging outfits, electronic calculators, pens, pencils, and cans of tennis balls, all emblazoned with the name of Lo-An or CHA-ZAH! in combination with a bit of sly humor. The shirts and jogging suits all bear the name of the fictitious Lo-An Yacht Club, located in nonexistent Cape St. Jacques, Florida. The white plastic coffee mugs are inscribed "LOVE means never having to say sorry I ate the last CHA-ZAH!" and when you open a can of three vacuum-packed Dunlop tennis balls, you discover they're all imprinted with the words "CHA-ZAH! Designer Eggrolls."

Outstanding brokers can also receive a dinner certificate for two at a leading American Express restaurant, have a tailor measure them at home for a custom-made suit, and if they've done something really extraordinary, they and their wives will receive an all-expenses-paid cruise to the Caribbean. This gift-giving program, says Nguyen, "works very well, makes for good human relations, and is extremely cost-effective." So much so that it has been extended to Lo-An Delicacies' own employees as a reward for exceptional performance.

Chris and Lo-An also design the company's packaging with the help of a graphic artist, and write the copy appearing on it, including the letter from Lo-An which begins "Dear Friends," lists three different ways to cook CHA-ZAH! eggrolls, asks consumers to let them know what they think of the product, and ends with "Have a nice day."

"We get three or four letters a day from our customers," says Chris Nguyen, "and we answer each one personally." One customer suggested that microwave cooking instructions be printed on the box, and this will be done on the one that will hold a new generation of CHA-ZAH! eggrolls made without flavor-enhancing monosodium glutamate or preservatives.

Getting rid of these chemical additives, Nguyen says, will give his eggrolls a leg up on the competition, and the scientific importance of their absence will be explained in a letter on the package signed by Lo-An, who is a registered pharmacist.

These new eggrolls are part of Nguyen's grand strategy for doubling his sales. He's also purchased five acres of land a few minutes away from his present location, on which he plans to build a $1-million, 30,000-square-foot manufacturing plant. This new facility will allow Nguyen to meet rising demand for his CHA-ZAH! eggrolls, while bringing out new products such as chow mein, egg foo yung, and chicken teriyaki.

Chris and Lo-An Nguyen are well on their way to doing something that an estimated 95 percent of all American entrepreneurs never do—build a business with twenty or more employees.

The reasons for Lo-An Delicacies' growth are not difficult to find. It has a brand-name product that can move easily through existing distribution channels to consumers in all fifty states. Chris and Lo-An are natural managers who know how to get the best out of the people who work for them. They have additional—and complementary—products moving down the pipeline, along with a major new plant capable of manufacturing them in quantity.

This raises a question. Why can't the vast majority of entrepreneurs, who never reach takeoff velocity, simply follow in Chris and Lo-An Nguyen's footsteps? Several answers spring immediately to mind:

1. Most entrepreneurs don't want to do the backbreaking work it takes to build and manage a multimillion-dollar business. A smaller, less demanding business grossing $500,000 or less a year can give them a very comfortable life-style with plenty of free time for leisurely afternoons on the golf course.
2. Most entrepreneurs pursue business concepts that do not easily lend themselves to growth—barbershops, sod farms, filling stations, and bookstores. These businesses are establishments—as opposed to products capable of moving easily through familiar channels of distribution—and just about the only ways they can grow are through the following methods:

- Expanding the original establishment, as Grossinger's has done so successfully in New York and Knott's Berry Farm has done even more successfully in California.
- Cloning the original establishment through company-owned or franchised units; this has catapulted Culligan, Western Auto, Ramada Inns, and McDonald's into the big time, and is moving quite a few other entrepreneurs in the same direction (we'll meet one of them in a minute).
- Using the original establishment's famous name to launch a line of products, as New York's Chock Full o' Nuts has done with its "heavenly" coffee, which can be purchased from coast to coast.

3. Most entrepreneurs can't manage, let alone inspire the large number of people it takes to build a major business. In 1956,

Dr. William Shockley, who won the Nobel Prize for coinventing the transistor, launched the Shockley Semiconductor Laboratory, which employed eight of the most awesomely talented engineers the electronics industry has ever seen. But Shockley couldn't manage the likes of Robert Noyce, Gordon Moore, Shelton Roberts, and Eugene Kleiner, who left and shortly thereafter started Fairchild Semiconductor, Intel, and other epic Silicon Valley companies, as Shockley's venture weakened and eventually died.

4. Most entrepreneurs lack the strategic planning ability needed to build a major business. "When we had sales of $3 million," says George Hatsopoulos, chairman of Thermo Electron Corporation in Waltham, Massachusetts, "I was already looking forward to the day when we'd reach $100 million. When we hit $30 million, I began thinking about what we'd do when we got to $1 billion."

5. Most entrepreneurs have difficulty introducing an uninterrupted stream of new products, which, as we have seen, is the key to growth in any business. At the top of the list of new-product experts is Martin J. Friedman, creator and editor for the past two decades of *New Product News*, published by New York's Dancer Fitzgerald Sample advertising agency. Friedman is jovial, irreverent, reads voraciously, is a walking encyclopedia of new-product lore, attends countless trade shows, and never visits a strange town without prowling around local supermarkets in search of new products that may have slipped through his net.

Far more new products are being introduced today than ever before, says Friedman, with most falling into the category of food, drug, or cosmetic items retailing for $2 or less. The majority of new products are "line extensions" of already successful brands, and most of these are nothing more revolutionary than new flavors or fragrances, such as Butter-Flavored Crisco or Spice Scent Right Guard.

Growing Your Own Cigars

But the marketing creativity of America's leading new-product innovators doesn't stop at mere "line extensions," as even a casual reading of Friedman's *New Product News* makes clear. Three examples:

Health-oriented new products, which Friedman describes as the most important development to come along in years. Although many of today's new vim-and-vigor products are old brands reconstituted to be salt-free, caffeine-free, sugar-free, low-cholesterol, high-fiber, and the like, many more are genuinely new, such as the explosion in body/mind-improving audiotape cassettes ("Letting Go of Stress"), and high-tech exercise equipment (Gravity Gym, on which you hang upside down like a bat).

Do-it-yourself new products, such as Grecian Delight Gyros ("Each package contains the ingredients to make four authentic Greek pita bread sandwiches"), and a $9.95 grow-your-own "Tobacco Kit" containing "seeds for fifty plants, a self-watering greenhouse system and seedling starter medium, plus a step-by-step tobacco-growing guidebook, including advice on how to make your own cigars."

Character-endorsed new products, such as those which are currently rejuvenating the more than $1 billion presweetened children's breakfast cereal business, in which old-timers like Cap'n Crunch are now being elbowed aside by youngsters such as Pac-Man, Donkey Kong, the Smurfs, and the ubiquitous Strawberry Shortcake.

Most new products fail, and Friedman keeps a list of great supermarket flops—the food-and-drug equivalents of the Edsel, the Nehru jacket, and Smell-O-Vision. Over the years, says Friedman, "the consumer has voted against," among others:

- Flavored margarine. "Lever and Kraft knocked themselves out with strawberry-flavored margarine, chocolate-flavored margarine; the concept was just spread the margarine on a piece of toast and you've got an instant Danish pastry, but consumers rejected it."
- Artificial bacon. "General Foods keeps experimenting with this product, but has yet to create a winner."
- Canister-packed potato chips, such as Procter & Gamble's impeccable but costly Pringles. "It turned out that consumers really preferred plain old irregular potato chips with dark brown spots, that broke easily."
- Pop wines. Products such as Ripple and Annie Greenspring. "For a while it looked like they were going to take over the wine business."
- Flavored catsup. "Heinz tried Mexican-flavored and barbecue-flavored catsup, but consumers still prefer ordinary tomato catsup."
- Peanut butter and jelly in the same jar. "What a great idea, but it flopped."
- Frozen soups. "Campbell's, who should know the soup business better than anyone else, has failed a couple of times with this product, but hasn't given up and is currently testing a new line."
- Snack desserts. "Like chocolate pudding in little cans. This one started off strong, but, like so many others, faded a year or so after it was introduced."

Friedman figures that all a new product has to do to succeed is sell one case a week in the nation's top supermarkets. Sounds easy. Yet only a handful of blockbuster products, such as Campbell's tomato soup, Hellmann's mayonnaise, or Frito-Lay's Nacho Cheese Doritos, manage to do it.

"What it really takes to create a successful new product," says William J. McDonald, Frito-Lay's New Products Marketing Director, "is a thorough understanding of consumers' wishes, wants, and desires." The next steps, says McDonald, "are to articulate this potential demand in terms of a concept for a new product, test the concept with consumers, develop a product which fulfills the concept (which can take from six months to a couple of years), and if consumer response is positive, put it into production." Any new product's chance of success, needless to say, will be considerably enhanced if it has the kind of marketing muscle behind it that's made Nacho Cheese Doritos a $500-million-a-year cash cow, putting it into the winner's circle with other megaproducts like Valium, Jell-O Pudding, and Crest toothpaste.

One of the sensational attributes of a Nacho Cheese Doritos, or any other successful supermarket product, as Martin Friedman loves to point out, is that its life cycle can run for years. Swift bacon, Wrigley chewing gum, Goodyear tires, Prince Albert pipe tobacco, Sherwin-Williams paint, Gillette razors, Ivory Soap, Campbell's soup, Gold Medal flour, Lipton tea, and Carnation canned milk, for example, have been the leading brands in their fields for more than sixty years. Compare this with infinitely sexier high-technology products, from personal computers to videogames, which can wind up in the boneyard in a matter of months.

Reviving Tired Products

Before we leave new-product failures, it's worth noting that worn-out products that may be headed for retirement, if not the grave, can be revived, according to marketing experts at New York's Cadwell Davis Partners, an advertising agency that prides itself on its strategies for restoring tired products to robust good health. For example:

- Does the worn-out product have new uses? Arm & Hammer Baking Soda sales rose sharply after the product was promoted for freshening refrigerators.

147

- Is there a broader target market? Procter & Gamble reversed Ivory Soap's declining sales by advertising it for adults, rather than just for babies.
- Can it be sold in a more convincing way? Procter & Gamble's Pampers disposable diapers, which were only a so-so success when sold as a convenience item for mothers, took off like a shot after ads were changed to emphasize that they kept babies dry and happy.
- Is there a trend to exploit? Dannon Yogurt sales exploded after the product was linked to consumers' interest in improving their health.
- Can the product's distribution channels be expanded? Hanes did this when it packaged its "L'Eggs" panty hose in containers resembling rainbow-colored ostrich eggs, and displayed them on tall revolving stands strategically placed near supermarket checkout counters.

Selling more of the company's original product, prolonging its life through constant improvements, and introducing or acquiring a continuous parade of new products are at the heart of every successful business strategy.

Giant international corporations and small neighborhood entrepreneurs, needless to say, go about doing this in very different ways. This was driven home to me not too long ago, when I visited Coca-Cola's twenty-six-story corporate headquarters in Atlanta, and on the way back to my hotel stopped off at a convention of paint and wall-covering retailers.

Coca-Cola was in the process of spending millions on its new "Coke Is It" campaign to increase the sales of what may be the world's most successful product, sold through approximately 1,400 licensed bottlers in more than 155 countries, and would shortly add Hollywood films to its product line by purchasing Columbia Pictures for $1 billion.

The capital-poor paint and wall-covering store owners, on the other hand, were looking to motivational speakers and idea-sharing workshops to send them back home charged up with the sales-generating power of positive thinking.

Keynote speaker Joe Charbonneau, president of The Performance Group in Dallas, got a standing ovation following his talk entitled "Look Who's Wrecking Your Company Now," which contained the following advice:

- Watch what the competition is doing, and then do it better.
- Just think of how often you call customers who are causing you trouble, and how infrequently you call those who are the trouble-free backbone of your business.
- The only person in the world who will never leave you is you. So think and act like a winner.

The most popular of the idea-sharing workshops was one on "Generating Paint Sales"; its two chief insights were these:

- Industrial companies are continually painting their buildings and equipment, yet 85 percent of this vast maintenance market is not called on regularly by paint sellers.
- Nearly 70 percent of all exterior paint sold in America last year was sold at sale prices. So if you want to sell more paint, hold more sales.

Price-cutting sales are vital to the growth of most retail businesses, and there's virtually no limit on how often you can hold them. The Pottery Barn chain of glassware-to-home-products supermarkets runs a sale nearly every month of the year: a get-organized sale, a summer sale, a back-to-school sale, a Christmas sale, and so on, with each one requiring mass buying and months of planning. Bad weather or anything else unexpected can ruin a sale, and since prices have already been slashed, additional cuts aimed at attracting stay-at-home customers could result in serious financial losses.

Any retail outlet's sales personnel can contribute mightily

to its growth if they know the merchandise, and love to sell. If you've got one or two people like that working for you, anything is possible. Possibly the greatest example of this going is Joe Girard, who works for a General Motors dealer in Detroit and has been enshrined in *The Guinness Book of World Records* for selling 1,425 cars and trucks in a single year.

Making outside sales calls on old and prospective customers, as the paint sellers were urged to do, is another vital (if increasingly expensive) way of generating growth. A McGraw-Hill group keeps close track of the cost of an average sales call, which it has seen climb from $9.02 in 1942 to $205.40 in 1983, when it did its last survey. Keeping even a small sales force in the field is expensive, which is why so many businesses rely on direct marketing which can be a very cost-effective way of selling products and services. Direct marketing is selling straight to prospects (including other businesses), with your sales message delivered via the U.S. Postal Service, a telephone "communicator," or the media (print, radio, or television). The response to your sales pitch can be measured with considerable accuracy, and orders generated by it can be delivered directly to buyers' homes by mail, United Parcel Service, and so forth, or customers can carry the merchandise away themselves if it's available in a store such as Sears, whose catalog is the Big Mama of direct marketing.

To succeed in the direct-marketing business, it helps to have a prescreened list of likely prospects, a carefully pretested sales proposition, inspired pricing, and a good gimmick to get the target customer to respond to your offer. Mail-order companies, for example, regularly spend fortunes on marketing campaigns designed by masters of this exotic selling medium. There are mail order experts, for example, who believe that your chances of having prospects react favorably to your offer will be measurably increased if you can get them to remove a sticky paper token from one card and paste it down in a circle marked "YES" on another card. Other experts believe a higher price can sometimes spark the sales of a tired product, as Rodale Press learned when it boosted the cost of its old faithful *Family Encyclopedia of Common Illnesses* by 25 percent and saw its sales jump by 14 percent. You can learn many of these secrets by hiring a direct-mail firm to prepare your campaign, or you can try doing it yourself by consulting one of the many instructive books in the field such as *Elements of Direct Marketing* by Martin Baier or *The Direct Marketing Handbook.*

You'll also need a good product to succeed in direct mail, and it's a decided plus if you can dream up one that's a little bit off the beaten track, such as an "Authentic French Chef's Outfit," "Lifetime Pocket Screwdriver," or gloves to protect your hands from inkstains when reading a newspaper.

Mail-Order Ant Farms

In his book *How I Made $1,000,000 in Mail Order* E. Joseph Cossman says you've got to have three by now familiar characteristics to succeed in mail order, and one not so familiar. The first three are the ability to conceive a new product, spot emerging trends in the marketplace, and persevere when the going gets tough. And the fourth characteristic is the ability to write good advertising copy, or hire someone who can do it for you.

Cossman's writing style shines through in the copy for his hugely successful Ant Farm, consisting of a year's supply of ant feed, California sand, ant watcher's handbook, stock certificate for a generous supply of ants and so forth, packed in a plastic box about the size of an unabridged dictionary. "HERE'S AN ANT'S ENTIRE WORLD! Watch them dig tunnels—see them build rooms—marvel as they erect bridges and move mountains before your very eyes. Ants are the world's tiniest engineers . . . and seeing them plan and construct their intricate highways and subways is fascinating. But they do much more than that! Through the clear plastic walls of your ANT FARM you can see the ant soldiers guarding the roads . . . the laborers carrying their loads . . . the supply corps storing away food for the rest of the colony. Yes, the ANT FARM is actually a LIVING TV SCREEN that will keep you interested for hours."

You don't, by the way, have to be a $150,000-a-year copywriter working for a big Madison Avenue ad agency to create memorable words that sell. In his book *Confessions of an Advertising Man,* the great David Ogilvy applauds the following gem written by a dairy farmer:

> *"Carnation Milk is the best in the land.*
> *Here I sit with a can in my hand.*
> *No tits to pull, no hay to pitch.*
> *Just punch a hole in the son-of-a-bitch."*

One business that's used direct mail with great effectiveness is the London Wine Company of Brookline, Massachusetts, which saw its sales increase by just over 30 percent yearly after it started using the technique, and is now shooting for 50 percent annual growth. Owner Stephen Garber, who took over the thirty-eight-year-old family business in 1983, started out with a monthly newsletter that did poorly in attracting customers, but hinted at the selling power of direct mail. Garber's breakthrough came after he paid more than $30,000 for a computer system, which manages London Wine's direct-mail campaigns. It allows Garber to tailor his mailings to the known tastes of his customers, and keep track of every response. It's also attracting new customers to his store who enjoy fine wine and are willing to buy it in quantity when the price is right. One mailing to three hundred prospects for a five-dollar bottle of white Bordeaux, for example, resulted in the sale of sixty cases. Direct mail is but one aspect of London Wine's continuing marketing effort, which Garber says ranges from wine tastings to "knocking on doors" to having salespeople "who have a genuine affection for wine and whose enthusiasm infects our customers."

A good direct-mail campaign will skim the cream off your prospect list, leaving those who read your sales pitch—but did not buy—softened up for a telemarketing campaign. Stephen Garber routinely uses telemarketing as a follow-up to direct mail, and for prospecting for new customers.

It's been estimated that telemarketing is used to sell $75 billion worth of cookbooks, well-drilling equipment, computer services, livestock identification tags, auto insurance, and other products to millions of customers at relatively low cost every year. "One telephone in the hands of a knowledgeable communicator can produce profit," said the late Murray Roman, one of America's top telephone salesmen and chairman of the Campaign Communications Institute in New York.

If telemarketing is used correctly, and if your product is not too expensive or complex, there's a good chance you can close a sale after every half-dozen or so carefully targeted phone calls to prospective customers. The key, of course, is doing it right, a process that Roman described in his book *Telemarketing Campaigns That Work!*

All successful telemarketing campaigns begin with a good list of prospects, and there's no better list than your present customers, especially those who have bought from you by telephone before. These customers are even more important if they have credit cards, since all you have to do—once they've accepted your order—is to add the new charge to their accounts for payment through Visa, American Express, or whatever.

There are circumstances, according to Roman, when you can justify the cost of renting one of the more than 200,000 lists of cold-turkey prospects from a mailing-list company found in the Yellow Pages. One such occasion is when the profit margin on the order is large enough to support the cost of untargeted prospecting; another is when the product is something customers may keep buying over their lifetimes, such as membership in an auto club.

One interesting fact unearthed during a telemarketing campaign that Roman conducted for the Louisiana National Bank is that a product sold personally over the phone can often command a considerably higher price than a roughly similar one sold through the mails—33 percent more in the case of a credit-card-protection service offered by the bank.

Once you're decided to launch a telemarketing campaign, there are a number of ways you can make it more effective, as Montgomery Ward learned when building its Auto Club. Ward's signed up more than a million members in the first three years its Auto Club was in existence, using the pulling-power of direct-mail advertising aimed at its charge-card customers. But as direct mail's selling power began to wane, Ward's discovered that half of its charge-card customers hadn't read its direct-mail Auto Club offer (a fact that was confirmed when 25,000 of them signed up for the club after seeing an ad for it in *TV Guide*). Ward's decided to try to reach these prospects through telemarketing, which produced more than 150,000 new club memberships in one year.

Ward's quickly learned that several versions of any telemarketing sales pitch should be pretested before making a final selection, that the chosen version should be retested periodically to make sure the marketplace hasn't changed, and that even those telemarketing prospects who didn't sign up for its Auto Club were not a total loss. "People who don't buy on the phone," said the president of Ward's Auto Club, "will buy more in [our] retail and catalog stores, because they remember that Ward's thought enough to call and offer them something that they thought was a good buy for them."

The Yummy Yogurt Man

Retail stores like Ward's, ComputerLand, Ace Hardware, and countless others are the leading outlets for the cornucopia of new products emerging from the country's best entrepreneurial minds. They dominate the other half of the production/distribution continuum that drives the free-enterprise system from which winning entrepreneurs emerge. Winners from the distribution side of the equation use many of the same growth strategies as do the product creators, plus a few of their own, of which opening more stores is by far the most popular. Some retailers, like ComputerLand, sell their suppliers' products directly to customers, while others, like Kwik-Kopy, buy or lease these products for themselves and sell their output. Either way, the key to growth is opening more stores, and one entrepreneur who's doing this with gusto is Sheldon Fischer, owner of supermarkets, health-food restaurants, and ice cream parlors in and around Washington, D.C.

Fischer bought his first store near the University of Maryland shortly after the end of World War II, and turned it into a commissary selling bulk goods at near-wholesale prices to fraternity and sorority houses on credit. But the commissary proved to be a so-so business because Fischer couldn't turn over his inventory fast enough to make a decent profit. Fischer said he could have sold the business to a New York cabdriver who was eager to buy it for $15,000 or $20,000, but knew the cabbie couldn't make much out of it either, so he closed it down.

This experience pushed Fischer into supermarkets, which are a cash business where he could turn over his inventory—that is, stand to make a profit on his investment—more than four times a month, compared to about once every month and a half in the commissary. He eventually bought two supermarkets in Maryland and one in Washington, D.C., named them Best Food Stores, and, while keeping an eagle eye on this growing business, opened the first frozen yogurt stand in the nation's capital in 1976, christening it Yummy (Add culture to Your Life) Yogurt.

Fischer's two oldest sons were having trouble making a living around this time—one was a cinematographer, the other a college dropout—so he brought them into the business, running the Yummy Yogurt store. Pretty soon, says Fischer, the boys "started arguing over who's going to be the boss, so I figured I better get another store." Fischer signed a lease on a much bigger store, expanded the yogurt menu to include salads, sandwiches, quiche, soup, and so on, and was getting ready to open up when his cinematographer son decided to quit because he didn't "want to be in the fast-food business, standing behind a counter all day." This forced Fischer to hire an experienced store manager, who worked out so well that he hired another one to run a second Yummy Yogurt, and then one more to run a third, where Fischer has his office.

By now Fischer had things running so smoothly he decided to open a commissary to supply his Yummy Yogurt stores with hot foods he had been buying from someone else. His wife developed some recipes and trained the cooks, and once again Fischer hired a professional manager to run the operation. "We can manufacture our own hot foods cheaper than we can buy them," says Fischer, "and it gives us the option of changing our menus whenever we want to." Fischer then went back on the prowl for locations to open more Yummy Yogurt stores, and found a particularly good site in a building next to the house where Abraham Lincoln died. Fischer bought the building, opened his fifth Yummy Yogurt store, but then closed it a year later when someone offered to buy the building for a price he couldn't refuse.

Fischer then made a strategic error by opening a 5,000-square-foot "double-header" store with a Yummy Yogurt downstairs, a delicatessen upstairs, and its own cook and kitchen. "That store was so big and gave us so many problems," says

Fischer, "that we started looking for another location, which we found a block away in the Metro Market. This time we decided to open two Yummy Yogurt stands, which together took up only eight hundred square feet, yet did 70 percent of the business of the 5,000-square-footer and were more profitable."

Fischer got rid of the 5,000-square-foot "double-header," and immediately leased another one that was the same size, but was all on one level, and located in a section of Washington he felt was going to build up. "We called this store our 'Feastery,'" says Fischer, "because we gave it a menu that's more than just health foods. We started baking our own pizza, for example, and we gave the place an outdoor café that seats seventy people, with another 225 inside. I'm not crazy about Feastery operations, because the bigger they are, the tougher they are to control. But it's probably our highest-volume store and a profit-maker, and we're planning to open up some more here in Washington and Maryland."

Fischer's Yummy Yogurt operations began to be noticed, and before long, he was being written up in *People, The Wall Street Journal,* the *Washington Post,* and foreign publications. These articles started bringing in inquiries from people who wanted to buy Yummy Yogurt franchises, which Fischer turned down. "You have to do a franchise properly," says Fischer, "and we just weren't ready. I could have made a lot of money selling franchises, giving the people a little brochure, a book, or whatever, but no support. But I'm not a quick-buck artist and I like to sleep at night, so we said no until we were ready."

Fischer was nevertheless intrigued by the franchising idea because "it's a way to get more stores and expand quicker using the franchisees' money and our ability to show them how to run the business. So we now have a consulting firm and a lawyer helping us put a franchising package together. We also plan to support our franchisees. We'll put them into one of our Yummy Yogurt stores here in Washington that's like the one they're going to operate at home, and we'll teach them everything they need to know." One of the things they'll learn from Fischer is the importance of hiring and motivating people, which isn't easy in the fast-food business, where workers are usually young, unskilled, and low-paid. "These type of people," says Fischer, "change jobs frequently, don't show up for work, and if anything will make you an old man before your time, it's being harassed every day by labor problems. We try to do better for our people than the average fast-food place like Wendy's or McDonald's by giving them a full day's work instead of part-time. We also give 'em holidays, paid vacations, we try to promote from within, but we still have problems. I get managers of our Yummy Yogurt stores calling me up all the time saying two people didn't show up today and I'll be shorthanded, so I'll have to juggle some people to get him help. But if somebody doesn't show up for work at a franchisee's store, that's his problem. He can't call me to get that extra help, he's got to depend on himself, and that's the difference."

Two things that Fischer's franchisees will receive are Yummy Yogurt mix and supervision, which Fischer believes will put a considerable drag on the earnings of his franchise operation until it reaches a critical mass of franchisees. "If we franchise five Yummy Yogurt stores in Virginia," says Fischer, "we'll need someone to supervise those five stores. He might be able to supervise fifteen stores, but I'm still going to have to pay him to look after five. So to begin with, there's not going to be any bonanzas, but maybe my sons will benefit later on."

But Fischer isn't the kind of man who sits around waiting for things to mature. Like most successful entrepreneurs, he glories in making things happen, as he did recently when he bought the Real Rich Ice Cream Company, which has twelve franchised stores scattered throughout Washington, Maryland, and Virginia. "We took one of their stores," says Fischer, "renamed it 'Real Rich Cookies & Cream,' and are using it as the prototype for a new-look kind of store, because we think the present ones are obsolete. We're putting in different menus, baking cookies and muffins in these stores, putting in a snack corner which might sell hot dogs, sandwiches, bagels, or whatever because we don't think ice cream can make it all by itself. We'll probably have more franchises happening in Real Rich than in Yummy Yogurt, because it's a set and going franchise operation."

The steady expansion of Sheldon Fischer's fast-food business after several setbacks is typical of the growth patterns of successful enterprises. Most new businesses can't handle serious reversals, and quietly die. Dun & Bradstreet estimates that four companies simply pay off their creditors and disappear for every one that declares bankruptcy, and the National Federation of Independent Business puts this figure at an even higher ten disappearances for every bankruptcy.

Good management, however, can recognize no-win strategies early on, and quickly shift course toward more promising opportunities, thereby preserving the company's long-term growth.

9

Real Entrepreneurs Don't Quit

"Failures are skinned knees—painful, but superficial, and they heal quickly."

—H. Ross Perot,
Founder and Chairman,
Electronic Data Systems

Adam Osborne is a flamboyant, gutsy, self-confessed publicity hound whose Osborne Computer Corporation was born in 1981, did $92,789,000 worth of business in its fiscal year ended February 26, 1983, and six months later filed for bankruptcy in one of the most spectacular boom-and-bust dramas in recent American business history.

High-tech Silicon Valley companies like Osborne Computer are going belly-up all the time. There's nothing new about that. What sets Osborne Computer apart, however, is that its founder, Adam Osborne, is a professional writer who has coauthored a kind of syllabus for aspiring entrepreneurs, one that spells out the strategies he used to build his company into a spectacular overnight success, and reveals the mistakes that just as quickly brought it to its knees.

To be in business is to be assaulted by relentless adversity and crisis; it comes with the territory and no one is immune. But there are ways of coping, and in this chapter we'll look at strategies that Federal Express, Mary Kay Cosmetics, Winnebago Industries, Thermo Electron, and others have used to deal with setbacks. We'll hear from specialists in helping troubled companies. And we'll talk about survival philosophy with Bob Brennan, who has built his company—First Jersey Securities—into one of the fastest-growing brokerage firms in America. But first let's return to Adam Osborne and his chilling tale of *Hypergrowth: The Rise and Fall of Osborne Computer Corporation.*

Osborne begins his book with a full-page reproduction of a letter to his attorneys from a law firm representing the man who had come aboard as Osborne Computer's president and chief executive officer less than nine months before it declared bankruptcy. The letter warned Osborne that if his book libeled his company's ex-president in any way, both he and the publisher would be sued forthwith. This was enough to scare off one big-name publisher from bringing out Osborne's book, which is less than ecstatic about the management acumen of his company's ex-president. So Adam Osborne published the book privately.

Osborne's first business was a small publishing company he started in Berkeley, California, specializing in books about microcomputers. In 1972, Osborne was hired by General Automation to write a book about microcomputers called *The Value of Power,* and after that he wrote another one entitled *An Introduction to Microcomputers,* which he published himself. Osborne says he quickly sold ten thousand copies of his second book for four dollars apiece to a little outfit called IMS Associates, and that when sales of the book hit twenty thousand copies, and thirteen universities adopted the book sight unseen as a required text, Osborne knew he was on to something big.

Osborne kept on writing books about microcomputers, and by 1979 his company had twenty-five titles in print, which were generating sales of about $500,000 a year, when McGraw-Hill offered to buy him out. Osborne accepted, signing a contract to stay on managing the business for three more years. But he got itchy halfway through this contract, and began working on a concept for a new microcomputer to compete with Apple, Commodore, and Radio Shack, which virtually owned the personal computer industry in 1980. Osborne believed that Apple—not to mention IBM—was living proof that "to be number one, you don't have to be the best, you don't even have to be good. All that is necessary is that your product be adequate, properly supported, and readily available." This conviction led Osborne to design a personal computer containing everything necessary for low-cost computing, but excluding all extras. Then he decided to revolutionize the personal computer industry by making the "Osborne 1" portable, so that users could pick it up by the handle and carry it with them anywhere, even aboard an airliner, where it could easily be tucked under a seat.

Osborne started up his new business early in 1980 as a Subchapter-S Corporation named "Brandywine Holdings" while still working for McGraw-Hill. In the ensuing months, Osborne labored on his portable computer in his spare time, invested about $100,000 of his own money in start-up costs, brought in another $40,000 of venture money, and by the end of 1980 had a working prototype microcomputer of limited capability up and running. Osborne had also been assembling the nucleus of a management team to make and market his new computer, and by the end of 1980 he had hired a vice-president and general manager named Tom Davidson, with other key marketing and engineering executives following along in 1981.

The company was incorporated as Osborne Computer in the first days of 1981, and a few weeks after that its short, unhappy life got under way when it moved into a small, unfinished building in Hayward, California, and raised $900,000 of start-up capital. "In retrospect," says Osborne, "$900,000 was a pitiful sum—woefully insufficient to launch a project of Osborne Computer Corporation's magnitude . . . but [it] was all the money I could raise at the time."

Osborne immediately began assembling a top-notch board of directors, including Les Hogan, ex-chairman of Fairchild Semiconductor; Seymour Rubenstein, founder of MicroPro; Jack Melchor, a venture capitalist whose $40,000 was the first outside investment in Osborne Computer; and Richard Frank, the president of Sorcim and author of a popular computer program called SuperCalc.

Battering Vendors into Submission

The decision was made to announce the Osborne 1 at the West Coast Computer Faire in March 1981. The company's tiny engineering staff worked around the clock building a few prototype computers, the press was alerted (with four trade magazines featuring the still-untested Osborne 1 on their covers as the Faire opened), and a retail price of $1,795 was agreed upon. "At that price," says Osborne, "we would make a lot of money, providing Davidson could batter vendors into submission and buy parts for the aggressively low prices I had specified."

Osborne decided to get his little company noticed at the Faire by erecting a Plexiglas booth that soared toward the ceiling, with the company's "flying O" trademark shining from the top like a beacon. Within the booth was the by now highly publicized Osborne 1 personal computer, stuffed inside a heavy aluminum case. To make matters worse, text appearing on the Osborne's tiny viewing screen appeared to be rippling like ocean waves, which company employees manning the booth referred to as the "Hawaiian effect." Yet Faire-goers swarmed around Osborne's booth to see not only the world's first truly portable computer, but one priced at about half the cost of competing PCs. Osborne himself was so elated by his success that he hurled a challenge at the feet of Apple, Commodore, Radio Shack, and any other competitor with the temerity to adopt a different strategy from his own. "Do as I have done," thundered Osborne, "or perish!" This was too much for Apple's Steven Jobs, who grabbed the telephone, put in a call to Osborne, and, when told he was out, left the message, "Tell Adam he's an asshole."

Once the glory days of the Faire were over, it was time to deliver, and on June 30, 1981, the first Osborne 1 (serial number 000001) was shipped to Digital Deli in Mountain View, California. Osborne 1 sales were still going strong in the fall, thanks to superb publicity and advertising. Osborne says he orchestrated the media by helping trade press reporters write interesting articles about his new portable computer, and before long favorable stories began appearing in the national media, in *Time, Newsweek, The Wall Street Journal, Business Week,* and *Fortune,* and on "60 Minutes."

Osborne's initial two advertising campaigns were inspired. The first campaign, unveiled as the Osborne 1 was being readied for shipment, showed a picture of the product with the caption, "It was inevitable." The second campaign, launched after the Osborne 1 was in the hands of consumers, showed two businessmen obviously in competition with each other. The man on the left carried a briefcase, while the one on the right carried an Osborne 1. Beneath the two men was the simple caption, "The guy on the left doesn't stand a chance." The ads, says Osborne, "appealed directly to the fear of obsolescence so prevalent among professionals at that time. I backed it up on the lecture circuit," he adds, "where I would finish many public addresses by stating: 'If you work with numbers or words and you are not using a microcomputer, then you are working on borrowed time.'" Osborne Computer made another fundamental marketing decision at this time, and that was to bypass distributors and sell directly to computer dealers. Osborne put together a stellar network of dealers before shipping its first computer, and to keep the dealers happy it offered them profit margins of between 35 and 42 percent of the Osborne 1's listed retail price, and thirty days to pay.

Dealers who hadn't paid by the thirty-first day, however, lost 4 percent of their profit margin. All well and good. But in retrospect, Osborne believes "that the carefully designed dealer program had little if any impact on either product sales or dealers' early stampede to carry the Osborne 1. Dealers wanted the product simply because customers walked into their stores asking for it."

Osborne began shipping a few demonstration models to dealers in July 1981, with shipments of actual Osborne 1's totaling 612 units in August and 2,045 in December, the latter figure being fairly close to the projections in the company's business plan. In September the company posted its first million-dollar month, prompting Adam Osborne to crow that his company "was invincible."

Death Seventy-two Hours Away

While Adam Osborne's megalomania was in full flower, his company was suddenly struck by two life-threatening crises. Crisis number one occurred at 2:00 P.M. on Friday, September 4, 1981, when the Bank of America, alarmed by the sharp increase in Osborne's accounts payable (unmatched by compensating accounts receivable or computer shipments), announced that it planned to call in all the company's existing loans the following Monday morning. It appeared that the Osborne Computer Corporation would be dead within the next seventy-two hours, but over the weekend, board member Jack Melcher came up with $1.6 million in new money from investors who paid forty dollars apiece for shares of the company's Treasury stock, up from the $17.39 a share paid by those who had put in the earlier $900,000.

Crisis number two struck a month later, in October 1981, when the company was forced to order a general product recall. In its eagerness to get its product out the door and to bring in desperately needed cash, the company had shipped flawed computers that, in Adam Osborne's words, were "in need of six more months and a couple more prototype development rounds." The Osborne 1, although a smash hit with consumers, was suffering from nonexistent quality control.

Suddenly, mini-crises began popping up, most of them having to do with delayed product improvements that Adam Osborne had trumpeted to the press but couldn't deliver. "Euphoria," he says, "has a nasty habit of stumbling on reality." Red ink also threatened to reach flood stage with the company's accumulated deficit rising from $38,000 for the year ending November 29, 1980, to $1,320,000 a year later. Still, people kept buying the Osborne 1, forcing the company to move into a larger manufacturing plant.

While all this was going on, Osborne Computer began searching for customers overseas, and during those wonderful months of hypergrowth, export orders accounted for roughly 25 percent of its business. Osborne had its first $10-million month in August 1982, and in October it began shipping an upgraded version of the Osborne 1, which had double the original machine's data storage capacity, yet retailed for only $200 more. Osborne Computer's work force now totaled eight hundred, some first-rate executives had been recruited, new products were in the works, and underwriters began knocking on the company's door to see if it was interested in going public.

But the company's life-threatening problems refused to go away, and before long were joined by others. The success of the upgraded Osborne 1 cut into the sales of original machines, so that at one point ten thousand of them sat unsold on dealers' shelves. A second critical upgrading of the Osborne 1 so it could display a standard eighty characters per line on its viewing screen was delayed a year further, damaging the company's credibility. Serious problems with parts began surfacing. And an offer to upgrade any Osborne 1 belonging to a customer who wanted the increased capability turned into a fiasco that created rampant ill will in dealers.

Osborne Computer had been working on several new personal computers, but by the time 1983 rolled around, it was clear that it could only afford to introduce one—the IBM/PC-compatible Osborne "Executive," priced to sell for $2,495. Adam Osborne decided to blitz the dealers with a "lavish, one-week whistle-stop tour around the country, during which dealers would be feted with food, drink, and product demonstrations." The blitz worked, and at tour's end Osborne came away with approximately $25 million worth of orders for the Executive.

Wall Street continued to be interested in Osborne Computer, and the offers to take the company public kept coming in. In the second week of January 1983, Osborne Computer hired Robert Jaunich, the chief operating officer of Consolidated Foods in Chicago, to be its new president, replacing founder Adam Osborne. And on April 22, 1983, Jaunich and Osborne had a critical meeting in New York with representatives of Salomon Brothers, which had agreed to handle the sale of Osborne Computer stock to the investing public. Jaunich told the underwriters the company would lose about $4 million in its fiscal year ending February 1983, but in the next few days additional losses were uncovered, increasing the projected loss for fiscal 1983 to between $8 and $10 million, with an additional $10 million looming for the first quarter of fiscal 1984. "For Osborne Computer Corporation," says Adam Osborne, "it was the beginning of the end." The end came with the filing of bankruptcy on Tuesday, September 13, 1983.

Osborne Computer, however, did not die. It lives to this day in Spartan quarters in Fremont, California, where it recently emerged from bankruptcy and hopes to return to profitability during 1985. Adam Osborne is also back in the game with a new gig, Paperback Software International, which dreams of "acquiring rights to produce and market high-quality software products from independent software developers that lack the means of marketing their products on a nationwide basis."

"We constantly talk to the principals of failed firms, their bankers, and most of all the suppliers who've been left holding the bag, and what we find is that nine out of ten businesses fail because of bad management," says Joseph W. Duncan, economist and chief statistician for the Dun & Bradstreet Corporation, which pays closer attention to business failure than anyone else in America.

"What's especially surprising," says Duncan, "is that so many entrepreneurs have zero experience in the businesses they've started. A man may go into business because he's a great salesman, only to find that his Achilles' heel is production, which he knows nothing about. This is particularly true during recessions, when people are fired from their jobs and decide to start a marina or something because they enjoy that activity. Now I realize that people don't go into business for themselves unless they're fundamentally optimistic. But unless they're also realistic about the business they're going into, and unless they know what they're doing, they're bound to overextend their resources and get into trouble."

Advice from Bankers Trust

Joseph A. Manganello, Jr., executive vice-president and senior credit officer of New York's Bankers Trust Company, whose assets exceed $45 billion, says, "We find that lots of companies get into trouble because they try to break out into a growth pattern they can't manage. An owner might be great at managing a plant that's got five milling machines and turns out one thousand widgets a month. But you double that to ten machines running on two eight-hour shifts a day, producing two thousand widgets, and pretty soon the owner starts to lose control. He's got to eat and he's got to sleep, which means he can no longer walk around the plant talking to each machine operator by name, jiggling this and jiggling that to make sure things go smoothly. So he's got to hire a guy to run the second shift, build up inventory, hire a sales force to move the extra widgets, and before you know it he's in over his head."

Manganello manages a team of ten "workout" specialists he sends into troubled companies to try to save the business and, not incidentally, the money Bankers Trust has lent them. "Early recognition is the key to staying out of trouble," says Manganello. "It's just like sickness. If you're not feeling well, there's something wrong. Same thing in business. When your numbers start to move against you, get professional help right away. Different businesses have different kinds of early-warning signals that trouble is brewing. In service businesses, for example, it's the generation and collection of receivables. If bookings start to slide off, or if payment of receivables starts to slow up, that's a sign of trouble.

"What's essential is that you have good accounting help. You may not be able to afford a Big Eight accounting firm, nor should you settle for a one-man band. Your best bet would probably be a firm with three or four partners, and it's a big plus if they have some experience in your business, so you should shop around. Use your accountants as consultants, get them to review your numbers. It costs a little money, and there's a temptation to skimp on this fee. But to have your accountants come in and do a six-month book audit, and then talk to you about what they've found, is money very well spent— particularly if they uncover a problem either actual or impending.

"It's also important to let your bank know as soon as you've got a problem," says Manganello. "And don't worry that the bank will cancel your loan. I hate to say this as a banker, but banks are not in a position to cancel loans, they're in a position to *make* loans, that's how they make their money. All we want to know is that we're going to get paid back. The moment you've got a problem and may have trouble meeting your loan payments, pick up the phone and call your banker. Tell him the problem, because he might be able to help. Say we lent you $100 and you told me you couldn't make your payment because a big customer was slow in paying you. I might say to you, 'Why are we fooling around with this $100 loan? I'll give you a line of credit allowing you to borrow up to 80 percent of your receivables. It might cost you a little more in interest, but it will free up your cash, and you won't have to worry as much about collecting from your customers. I'll collect your receivables for you, if it gets down to that.' "

One crisis-prone company that Manganello helped to turn around is Mattel, whose Barbie Dolls, Hot Wheels, Masters of the Universe, and other inspired playthings have made it the world's premier toy company. But for years Mattel's great joy in life was buying businesses it had never managed before such as the Ice Follies, the Ringling Brothers and Barnum & Bailey Circus, Florida's Circus World amusement park, and the electronics game company Intellivision.

"Mattel is a great name in toys," says Manganello, "but it's been in trouble twice during the last twenty-five years. Why? Because they went into businesses they didn't understand, like electronics, in order to grow faster and keep their stockholders happy. Mattel should have gone into bankruptcy. But the company's senior management, which let the electronics thing happen and got one good year out of it, got in touch with their bankers early on. They told us, 'Look, this is what's going to happen. We don't know how bad the problem is, but it's so bad we can't pay back your loans.' We could have beaten our chests, pulled our hair out, but the fact was that Mattel didn't have any money to pay us off. But Mattel is a good name, and so what you do is put your workout guys in there and keep them in business so they can start selling toys again. The banks worked out a program where they took Mattel's debt schedule, got more collateral, put Mattel's loan repayments on a schedule they could handle with their projected cash flow, and provided them with seasonal financing. Mattel, for its part, did things it had to do. It got out of the electronics business, recognized its loss on the balance sheet, brought in new investors, and went forward. Mattel skirted the edge of corporate death and survived because its management immediately responded to their crisis, alerted their bankers, and worked with them. As for us, we got our money back in three years instead of one, but that's better than not getting it back at all." Mattel moved solidly into the black during the third quarter of 1984, a feat that company chairman Arthur Spear said "validates our decision to concentrate on the business we know best—the production, distribution, and marketing of toys."

Sooner or later, every company gets into trouble. But if it's got winning management and enough fat on its bones to give that management the time and resources it needs to put things right, then it can avoid the ultimate ignominy of corporate death. The managements of some of the best-known names in American business have gone through the fires of adversity and come out stronger than ever before.

Saving Winnebago Industries

Winnebago Industries of Forest City, Iowa, builds recreational vehicles, and in 1971 its stock soared 462 percent, making it the hottest company in the nation. Business was setting such a furious pace that ex–funeral director and furniture store owner John K. Hanson, who had purchased control of the company twelve years earlier, decided it was safe to retire to the Isle of Capri in Florida. Then came OPEC's quadrupling of world oil prices, and later the gas crunch, which dropped Winnebago's revenues from $229 million in 1978 to $92 million in 1980. Hanson says things got so scary that he began receiving calls in February 1979 from old-time Winnebago blue-collar employees warning him "the company was kaput and was about to go belly-up." So at age sixty-five, having just recovered from a cataract operation, Hanson returned to Forest City completely confident that he could save the company he had built. "There was nothing to it," Hanson says. "It's sort of like your wife who's made a lot of apple pies and knows she can make another one pretty easy."

The first thing Hanson did after taking back the reins at Winnebago was to reclaim the posts of chairman and CEO from his handpicked successor, J. Harold Bragg (and the presidency from his son, John V. Hanson, who resigned from the company the next day). Shortly thereafter, Hanson announced a belt-tightening program that slashed Winnebago's employment rolls from 3,250 to 800 people. "That was heartbreaking," says Hanson, "but I had to do it to save the company." Hanson also sold and consolidated several plants, and in the next eighteen months Winnebago went from $18.5 million in debt to $20 million in cash and negotiable securities.

Founder Hanson, however, wasn't finished yet. His big problem was that Winnebago's best-selling motor homes hadn't changed much since they were introduced in 1965, a fact that had consigned Winnebago to third place in the RV industry, after Coachman and Fleetwood. Winnebago motor homes only got eight to twelve miles to the gallon, and Hanson knew that if he didn't make them more fuel-efficient his business might go the way of three-dollar-a-barrel petroleum. Hanson's first step was to raise the Winnebago's fuel mileage by decreasing its weight and improving its aerodynamics. Then he went scouring the planet for a fuel-saving engine, which he finally found in a new diesel that Renault—France's number-one carmaker—had spent seven years and $2 billion developing. In mid-1982, Winnebago introduced a new line of small motor homes that got twenty-two-plus miles per gallon and sold for close to $20,000 instead of the more than $40,000 its older larger models had cost. Shortly thereafter it unveiled a badly needed full-size motor home that also scrimped on fuel.

Winnebago's turnaround was completed in 1984, helped along by a move into motor-home rentals, and the creation of a New Ventures Division "to lessen the company's dependence on energy-sensitive recreation vehicles." That division has already put Winnebago into the business of selling fabricated aluminum products and plastic garbage cans, and licensing the Winnebago name to manufacturers of coolers, backpacks, sailboats, and other products designed for the outdoors. Winnebago is once again reporting record sales and earnings, and seventy-one-year-old John Hanson, who was recently inducted into the RV/Motor Home Hall of Fame, is planning to retire again as soon as he finishes a plan "to preserve the long-range life expectancy of Winnebago Industries for the employees, the community, and the stockholders."

Crisis struck Fred Smith's Federal Express when the limited capacity of its small Falcon jets threatened to brake its expansion and sharply increase the cost of providing overnight package delivery service from its cargo-handling hub in Memphis. The company wanted to fly bigger, more fuel-efficient jets, but the Civil Aeronautics Board said it couldn't do this.

It was a potentially crippling blow to Federal Express, since its 1976 business plan showed that if it couldn't use bigger planes, its growth would grind to a halt within twenty-four months. This infuriated Smith, who, just three years after launching the business, had made it (1) the leading company in the small-shipment air-express market, and (2) profitable. "The government doesn't have to give us a thing," said Smith. "All they have to do is get out of our way."

Smith's next move, familiar to anyone who has ever taken on the Kafkaesque federal bureaucracy, was to go to Washington, enlist the aid of the Tennessee Congressional delegation, and hire legal counsel familiar with the internal workings of whatever government agency was giving his company grief. After months of intensive lobbying, the expenditure of a great deal of money, and numerous time-consuming appearances before House and Senate committees, Smith failed to get Congress to pass legislation allowing Federal Express to buy bigger airplanes. Smith, however, was not discouraged. "If you keep working at it," he said, "in the last analysis, you win. We're like old Ho Chi Minh. They've got to kill us one hundred times. All we have to do is kill them once."

Thanks to the work of Fred Smith and others, airline deregulation was now on Washington's front burner, and on November 9, 1977, President Jimmy Carter signed legislation making air cargo the first industry to be decontrolled by Congress. Federal Express could now buy any size airplane it wanted, and within weeks it had acquired a fleet of Boeing 727-100's, with an effective cargo capacity of 42,000 pounds apiece, compared to the Falcon's 7,500-pound payload. Federal Express was now free to become an entrepreneurial legend in its own time.

The crisis that hit Mary Kay Cosmetics two years ago was sparked by the nation's exuberant economy, which slowed the company to a crawl after a decade of turbocharged growth. The engine of Mary Kay Cosmetics' growth is its 194,000 or so independent beauty consultants, most of whom leave the company each year and must be replaced. The vast majority of Mary Kay's saleswomen work part-time, and it is much harder to recruit new ones when the economy is booming— and full-time jobs are fairly plentiful—than when times are tough. This fall-off in the company's recruiting rate, together with a decrease in the productivity of its sales force, and continuing high fixed overhead, cut deeply into Mary Kay's profits in 1984, slashed the price of Mary Kay Cosmetics' stock from a peak of nearly forty-five dollars a share, in May 1983, to nine dollars a share toward the end of 1984, and brought into question the prediction of company president Richard Rogers that Mary Kay's sales would hit $500 million by the end of this decade.

Rogers, who is Mary Kay Ash's son, acted to reverse this situation in late 1983 when he announced he had frozen corporate-level hiring, canceled an $8-million advertising budget, deferred the market-testing of new products, halted most building projects, and significantly beefed up incentive programs to attract and hold more beauty consultants. These strategic moves, plus the U.S. economy's turn toward slower growth, could put Mary Kay back on the track. "If the economic pendulum does swing back the other way," says Rogers, "guess what? We'll be there with bells on."

The Great Wild Card

The economy is the great "wild card" in business, and when it takes a turn for the worse, as it always does sooner or later, ineptly managed companies can get wiped out, and even expertly managed ones like Thermo Electron Corporation of Waltham, Massachusetts, can be sorely tested.

Thermo Electron is a recognized leader in the use of advanced technology to raise the efficiency of energy-intensive processes, such as the generation of electricity. The company was founded by its chairman and president, Dr. George Hatsopoulos, who is also a senior lecturer at MIT and a member of the board of directors of the Federal Reserve Bank of Boston. Hatsopoulos managed Thermo Electron like a Kentucky Derby winner, with sales and earnings per share growing by more than 25 percent a year throughout the sixties and seventies. Thermo Electron was one of the darlings of Wall Street; its business of helping its customers use energy more efficiently was given a boost by the same OPEC-induced energy crises of the seventies that clobbered Winnebago. But then disaster struck Thermo Electron in the guise of the severe 1981–82 recession, which slashed its sales and reduced its 1983 profits to the vanishing point. It was the worst recession in Thermo Electron's history, and it caught Hatsopoulos unawares, if not unprepared.

"Toward the end of 1981," says Hatsopoulos, "I thought there might be a modest recession, but nothing severe enough to hurt our business. Back then, everyone was bullish about the economy—the President, the stock market, the economists, everyone. To be honest with you, I don't think [Federal Reserve Board Chairman] Paul Volcker saw the recession coming before I did. But we have a philosophy at Thermo Electron which says we should always be prepared for the worst. I believe companies should take big risks on their profit-and-loss statement and go after big markets with big potential. But I don't believe they should ever take a risk on their balance sheet. Companies don't go bankrupt because they lose money on their P-and-L," says Hatsopoulos, "but only because they run out of cash, which shows up on their balance sheets. You could have a big write-off and show a huge loss, but as long as you've got cash, it doesn't make any difference except in the price of your stock. For years now, I've said let's manage our balance sheet so we could survive the Great Depression of the 1930s. Some of our people think I'm crazy. But I don't want to take the risk, even if there's only one chance in a hundred of it happening again. I have too much invested in this company."

Hatsopoulos realized Thermo Electron was in for trouble in February 1982, and quickly put two damage-control plans into action. The first involved routine decisions such as cutting Thermo Electron's work force by 20 percent, from 3,200 to 2,500 people. The second plan, however, was more far-reaching, involving nothing less than a fundamental restructuring of the company to improve its productivity.

"We had a list of things we wanted to do to streamline the company if business ever leveled off enough for us to reorganize," says Hatsopoulos, and when a "breathing space" finally arrived in 1982–83, he used it to consolidate six divisions into two, close four divisions serving no-growth markets, and sell one division in the United Kingdom outright.

Hatsopoulos had another tough call to make during this down period in the company's fortunes, and that was whether or not to go ahead with plans to substantially increase spending on research and development. Thermo Electron is a high-tech company building unique equipment, such as a $33-million advanced-design power plant for a municipal center in Dade County, Florida. This "co-generation" plant burns natural gas to produce 17,000 kilowatts of electricity, takes the exhaust heat from this plant and runs it through a steam turbine to produce another 5,200 to 8,200 kilowatts of power, takes the exhaust steam from this generator and uses it to produce air conditioning equivalent to between 1,100 and 5,200 tons of melting ice, and recycles the waste heat from this operation to produce three hundred gallons of hot water a minute. Since research and development is Thermo Electron's life blood, Hatsopoulos decided to accelerate R&D expenditures, concentrating on the "development of technology that we could sell in the first quarter of the recovery."

The recession also taught Hatsopoulos that he should never again allow Thermo Electron to "get involved with low-margin products somebody else can build," and that he should "focus on serving industries that are less susceptible to economic downturns, such as electronics and defense." One new product that fulfills both these criteria, and of which Hatsopoulos is justly proud, is the equipment for electroplating printed circuit boards like those that the Digital Equipment Corporation uses in its computers. "One form of this circuit board," says Hatsopoulos, "has thirty-five layers and 300,000 connections. Plating each layer—and doing it without an enormous rejection rate—requires a level of sophistication that goes beyond human capability and must be completely computerized." Orders for this new line of process equipment, says Hatsopoulos, "are flooding in."

While Hatsopoulos was pursuing this high-technology phase of his recovery strategy, he received a telephone call from the president of Peter Brotherhood Ltd. in England, which makes all of the turbines for Thermo Electron's co-generation systems. The president's message was short and to the point. "He told me," says Hatsopoulos, "that because of the terrible recession in Europe, his company was unable to meet its cash obligations and might have to go bankrupt, which would have been catastrophic for us." So in the midst of a recession that had practically destroyed Thermo Electron's 1983 profits, and with record R&D outlays further draining its cash resources, Hatsopoulos dug down into his still-strong balance sheet and shelled out $1,264,000 to buy Peter Brotherhood.

Hatsopoulos's grand recovery strategy worked. Thermo Electron's business continues to improve in all product areas, its order backlog is at record levels, and the increases in productivity made possible by the recession-induced "breathing space" are paying off in rising sales and profits. "The future," says Hatsopoulos, "looks very bright."

Strength Through Adversity

No discussion of dealing with adversity and crises would be complete without mentioning the one trait that, more than any other, seems to separate winners from losers in entrepreneurially driven businesses. It is that winners not only won't quit, but seem to gain strength from adversity. They keep coming back for more, they refuse to be beaten, and as a result they can usually stand up to almost anything the fates have to offer. Lisa M. Amoss, an adjunct professor at Tulane University's School of Business in New Orleans, estimates that winning entrepreneurs "average 3.8 failures before the final success. They just keep going," she says, "and I don't know how."

What Professor Amoss is talking about is personified by James U. Blanchard III whose company is headquartered in nearby Metairie, Louisiana. A car accident confined Blanchard to a wheelchair at age eighteen, but didn't stop him from building a thriving financial enterprise, and later founding the National Committee on Monetary Reform which every fall, for more than a decade, has sponsored the world's largest investment conference. This conference has been addressed by former presidents of the United States, Nobel Prize–winning economists, and the biggest names in the investment advisory business from Harry Browne to Martin Zweig.

One winner who has a philosophy about all this is Bob Brennan, a tall, handsome, forty-year-old blond man with steel-blue eyes who founded First Jersey Securities in 1973 and has since built his company into what he claims is the nation's fastest-growing brokerage firm, with some thirty-five offices, one thousand sales representatives, 400,000 customers, and assets of $250,000,000. Brennan lives in a palatial estate on the New Jersey shore, has had Vice-President George Bush as his house guest, owns more than three hundred thoroughbred race-horses, and can be seen on coast-to-coast television, urging investors to "come grow with us."

Bob Brennan grew up as one of eight brothers and sisters living in a tiny apartment in a rundown section of Newark, New Jersey. He began battling adversity at age ten, when he went into the candy business. "When I was a kid in Newark," says Brennan, "I met a man who had a wholesale candy store around the corner from me. He allowed me to take out shopping bags full of candy on consignment, which I sold to people sitting in the park. You see, I had this desire to work when other kids were playing, and the persistence to keep going even though sixteen people in a row told me, 'No, I don't want any candy today.' The lesson I learned back then was that although I had no money, I did have the ability to deal with people rejecting me, and creating all kinds of doubts and fears in my mind as to whether or not I was going to be successful.

"Probably the single most important characteristic that's helped me succeed is my ability to lose, and to deal with it properly. I've lost a lot more than I've won, but I've learned that losing doesn't make you a loser, any more than winning makes you a winner. The first thing you've got to do is accept the fact that if you're going to expose yourself to achieving something, then you are also exposing yourself to failing—and that failing is a perfectly acceptable consequence. Failing doesn't make you bad, it shouldn't lower your self-esteem, it simply means you've taken on additional exposure. One of my heroes when I was growing up was Babe Ruth, the Home Run King, who hit 714 homers during his career. As a kid that was all I knew about Babe Ruth. But I've since learned that Babe Ruth holds the record to this day for the most strikeouts of anybody in the history of major-league baseball. So it's not strikeouts that matter, it's how you respond to them. You could have somebody bang into your brand-new car as you're backing out of your driveway this morning. Is that a plus or a minus? Well, if you jump out of your car and start hollering and screaming at the person who hit you, and let that event ruin the rest of your day, then it is a minus. But if you got out of the car and said, 'Hi, I'm Bob Brennan, I'm sorry for your trouble, is there anything I can do to help you?' then that's a plus. You've relieved somebody else's anxiety, you've probably made a friend. You've built a little bit of character, and you've improved your self-control. In other words, if you hadn't started your day with an accident, you would have lost an opportunity to grow individually, spiritually and emotionally. So the event was good.

"It's like lifting weights. If your ambition is to lift five-hundred-pound weights, then the first time you walk into the weight room and lift fifty-pound weights, you'll probably go home that night with sore muscles because they're the first weights you've ever lifted. But you can't look at those fifty-pound weights as your enemies because they've inflicted pain on you. They did inflict the pain, but they're your friends, because in the absence of the fifty-pound weights you can't get to the hundred-pound weights, and in the absence of the hundred-pound weights you can't lift the still heavier weights you must master to reach your goal. This is the way we grow as people."

You must be willing to work gruelingly long hours and take substantial risks if your goal is to join that select circle of entrepreneurs who have made it big in a growing and profitable business of their own. "I find that if I work sixteen to eighteen hours a day I get lucky," says Armand Hammer, founder and chairman of the Occidental Petroleum Company, whose sales topped $15 billion in 1984. And as to risk, Walter Wriston put it this way right before he stepped down as chairman of Citicorp, which he helped build into the nation's largest bank holding company, with assets in excess of $150 billion. "If wages come from work, rent from real estate, and interest from savings—where do profits come from? The answer is that profits come from risk. The essential difference between the bureaucrat and the entrepreneur is the willingness to take risks."

10

The Big Winners

"We're not here for gold watches—we're here for greatness."

—Jerry Sanders,
Chairman, Advanced Micro Devices

In the rough-and-tumble world of free enterprise, only a handful of super entrepreneurs ever succeed in building a business with sales of $25 million a year or more.

More fledgling entrepreneurs are stopped dead in their tracks by their failure to navigate one of the eight steps they must take if they are to get from burning desire to be their own boss, to the promised land of owning a moneymaking business of their own. Perhaps they failed to come up with (1) a winning concept; (2) a sound view of the future; (3) a workable business plan; (4) sufficient capital; (5) key nonfinancial resources, from good people to dependable suppliers; (6) a successful strategy for launching the new business into the marketplace and (7) expanding it once it got there; or (8) resources for overcoming the adversity and crises to which every business is eventually heir.

The sad truth is that while most new businesses fail, a distressingly large number just poop along, going nowhere for years on end because their owners don't know how to break out into the big time. Only about 15,000 U.S. companies have yearly sales of $25 million or more, and less than five hundred have sales in excess of $1 billion.

Until quite recently, we paid little attention to the strategies that winning companies use to grow and prosper. But then, in 1982, a book called *In Search of Excellence: Lessons from America's Best-Run Companies* was published, which quickly became the best-selling business book in history. More than five million copies have been sold to buyers interested in learning the coauthors' secrets for business success, which boiled down to: make sure your company stands for something worthwhile; never be afraid to act; stay close to your customers; stick to your knitting; take good care of your employees, and encourage them to act like entrepreneurs; and run a tight ship, but not so tight that you discourage innovation.

Tips from the Big Winners

A year after *In Search of Excellence* hit the *New York Times* best-seller list, the management consulting firm of McKinsey & Company delivered another study on company excellence to Jack Albertine, president of the American Business Conference in Washington, D.C., which had commissioned it two years earlier. The study was called *The Winning Performance of the Midsized Growth Companies,* and it was based largely on interviews with the leaders of sixty ABC member companies with sales of between $25 million and $1 billion, and at least a 15-percent annual growth in sales or profits for five years straight. Albertine says even the smallest entrepreneur can profit from these midsized companies' strategies for growth, of which four stand out from the rest:

Innovate as a way of life. No less than 74 percent of the winning companies surveyed by McKinsey said they had achieved their first big success with either a unique product or a distinctive way of doing business (although this break-through may not have come along until they had been in business for many years). Sixty-one percent of the companies attributed their current success to innovation (noting that this becomes harder to achieve as you grow larger), while the respondents as a whole said that more than 25 percent of their sales were being generated by products less than five years old.

Lead in niche markets. These must be cultivated so that the companies won't have to take on giant competitors for whom such markets may be of only marginal interest. Sixty-six percent of the respondents said that more than half of their sales come from niche markets in which they have a leadership position, and nearly 80 percent get at least a quarter of their sales from this source.

Build on strength. Companies grow by doing more of what they're good at, from introducing unique products, to capitalizing on a well-established name, to responding quickly to customer needs. They also use these strengths to move out of profitable but fading niches and into more promising related ones. This same strategy of building on strength is used in acquiring other companies, which are almost always in businesses where they already have an edge. If these winning firms are forced to alter their direction, they will try to do it from strength, like one respondent company that used its knowledge of the newspaper business to enter the related but far larger business of communications services.

Compete on value rather than price. Eighty-one percent of the respondents said their products were superior to the average for their industry, and 56 percent said they were the highest quality available. The study noted that midsized companies turning out top-quality products had a four-year return on investment averaging 60 percent higher than companies producing ordinary products, and that companies whose products lead in value are often the lowest-cost producers.

Winning ABC member companies such as Dunkin' Donuts, Levitz Furniture, and California Portland Cement have other qualities in common, according to the McKinsey study. They share a strong sense of mission and values, pay close attention to business fundamentals such as the need for sophisticated financial control systems, fight bureaucracy, encourage experimentation, try to think like their customers, and put top priority on developing and motivating good people. Fast-growing companies are capitalism's champions, and although they have a great deal in common, no two ever travel exactly the same road to the top. This can be graphically demonstrated by the strategies pursued by three winning companies in the totally different businesses of telecommunications, defense consulting, and cowhides:

- MCI Communications Corporation in Washington, D.C., a capital-intensive business run by its hard-charging chairman and founder, whose brand-new multibillion-dollar telecommunications network already serves some two million customers, won in head-to-head competition with mighty AT&T.
- BDM International in McLean, Virginia, is a people-intensive "knowledge business" founded by three physicists, but run by a professional manager, which gets 86 percent of its revenues from contracting with the U.S. military on projects such as the vaunted "Star Wars" system for protecting America against Soviet nuclear missiles.
- The Seton Company of Newark, New Jersey, traces its roots back to 1906, when the immigrant grandfather of its present chairman co-founded a leather-tanning business that is being used today as a "cash cow" to lever it into new, faster-

growing businesses, from industrial adhesives to health-care products.

Bill McGowan's MCI

MCI Communications is headed by William G. McGowan, fifty-seven, a chain-smoking, workaholic bachelor who came out of nowhere to build the nation's second-largest long-distance telecommunications network after AT&T. McGowan is a product of the Pennsylvania coalfields who found his way to Cambridge, Massachusetts, and the Harvard Business School. With his Harvard degree in hand, McGowan went to work for Hollywood impresario Mike Todd, then struck out on his own by starting up several little companies, including one that built testing devices. McGowan sold this business in 1967, and a year later, while on a business trip to Chicago, stumbled upon the concept that, fifteen years later, gave him a net worth in excess of $30 million.

McGowan's concept came to him via one John D. Goeken, who owned a company called Microwave Communications, and five years earlier had applied to the Federal Communications Commission in Washington, D.C., for a license to erect a microwave system between St. Louis and Chicago. AT&T was fighting Goeken's proposal, arguing that in addition to everything else he lacked the money to build such a system, which turned out to be correct. McGowan got Goeken to let him pay off MCI's debts and manage its business, which he promptly moved to the nation's capital, where he planned to do battle with the FCC and anybody else who got in the way of his turning tiny MCI into a communications powerhouse.

McGowan's first strategic decision was not to buy MCI, since any change in its ownership would delay its application for a St. Louis–Chicago microwave license by another five years. McGowan decided it was better to end-run the FCC by setting up seventeen regional companies and having each of them apply for permission to build a leg of a national microwave network. The strategy worked, the FCC approved all seventeen applications, and McGowan raised $7 million to finance his babies; he then tucked them into Microwave Communications, Inc., which he had since acquired from Goeken.

By 1972, McGowan's MCI consisted of a series of slim microwave towers twenty-two miles apart, which relayed phone messages from point to point throughout much of the United States. McGowan began offering high-volume business users private-line telephone service between any two points on MCI's system, which they could rent by the month at prices significantly below what AT&T was charging. It wasn't long before AT&T struck back at this intrusion into its long-distance telephone preserve by, according to McGowan, unplugging some needed phone connections and slashing prices on selected long-distance routes.

AT&T's counterpunching, along with the traditionally low profit margins on private-line telephone service, was hitting MCI with millions in losses, and by mid-1975 McGowan was on the ropes. So he shifted his strategy and decided to go for broke by attacking AT&T's highly profitable, highly vulnerable long-distance telephone business. What McGowan knew—and nobody else, including the FCC, seemed to realize—was that although the states had given AT&T a clear monopoly in the local areas it served, no one had given it a monopoly on long-distance service.

McGowan jumped on this oversight by introducing MCI's cut-rate Execunet long-distance telephone service. The FCC ordered MCI to cease and desist, and McGowan retaliated by taking AT&T to court. Three years later, in 1978, the Supreme Court decided in McGowan's favor, although by this time lackluster business and towering court costs had turned MCI's balance sheet into something McGowan says "looked like Rome after the Visigoths had finished with it. We had a $90-million negative net worth, and we owed the bank $100 million, which was so much that they couldn't call the loan without destroying the company."

At one point in his career, McGowan was a consultant who specialized in helping troubled companies, and one of the things he observed was that "a lot of people didn't know what the hell business they were in. They had misidentified what they should be doing, what their purpose was in life." McGowan hasn't been troubled by this problem.

"What we've had to do," says McGowan, "is succeed in a lot of different businesses. When we first came here to Washington, we were in the raising-venture-capital business. We succeeded in that business. Then we went into the next one, which was lobbying the government to get permission to go into business. We succeeded in that business. Then we raised a lot of money and went into the long-distance telephone business, which I thought we'd be in forever. It turned out we were only in that business for two years, because AT&T thought we should be in another business. So we went into the business of battling in the courts for the absolute right to provide the services we wanted to provide—while surviving in the interim. We succeeded in that business, and went into the one we're in today." Within two years after MCI had won its court battles, the company's sales force—working on nothing but commissions—had signed up 41,000 business customers, and was going flat out to sell MCI's Execunet services to residential customers. This triggered MCI's explosive growth phase as it enlarged and upgraded its network, added more customers (with the help of a computerized telemarketing center, which called more than 1.5 million potential new customers each month), and kept introducing new products for these customers to buy.

MCI's domestic communications network currently covers more than 20,000 route-miles and is growing daily. Its original forest of spindly microwave towers has been augmented by miles of hair-thin fiber optics, which can carry virtually unlimited amounts of information, and by transponders on earth-orbiting satellites, which are helping MCI expand its communications services to customers throughout the world. MCI's low-cost telephone services are now being used by some two million customers in the United States alone, and the company is rapidly increasing its ability to meet the data-carrying needs of computer users. MCI has also unveiled a parade of new products including mobile telephone service, electronic pagers capable of printing messages on their tiny display screens, and most recently MCI Mail, which can flash a message between computers thousands of miles apart in seconds for one dollar. "We are to the information world," says McGowan, "what transportation was to the industrial world. We are the transportation system of the future."

MCI is one of the truly incredible breakout stories of recent business history. Few companies have succeeded in doing what MCI has done against such overwhelming odds, and the credit belongs to the entrepreneurial dynamism of one man— Bill McGowan—whose strategic insights should be food and drink to anyone interested in building a great business.

McGowan works out of a cluttered corner office in MCI's downtown Washington headquarters, where he can be found alone on a typical weekend, enveloped in a cloud of cigarette smoke, with a copy of *Corporate Cultures: The Rites and Rituals of Corporate Life* open on his desk, worrying about the creeping bureaucracy he sees draining his company's life-force.

Beware the Money Spenders

McGowan wasn't troubled by this problem during the first five years MCI was in business, because the company had few employees and was highly centralized, with McGowan making all the decisions. "I had to," he says, "because I was afraid if I didn't, somebody would go out and spend money." But then MCI started its spectacular growth, employment boomed, and even McGowan couldn't stop it, as hard as he tried. "I thought when we moved into our headquarters building we should put a plaque on the wall reading, 'This is it, no more space, don't hire anybody we can't fit in here.' But even before we could get the plaque up, we were in four more buildings."

McGowan quickly realized that the only way to manage this kind of wildfire growth was to hire entrepreneurial-minded people who "would not chicken out on me, who would not begin saying, 'Oh, my God, how long do I have to keep putting in these twelve-hour days?' and begin to do self-limiting things such as installing all kinds of systems and procedures, which slows the company down, or blaming their own incompetence on some outside force such as technology or competition. We want hands-on managers who know everything that's going on in their operation. People who can identify the critical path— the most important things facing them—and then get those things done. That's what I do. I don't do anything else."

McGowan used to meet every Monday at 8:00 A.M. with those of his key managers who were in Washington. They'd go around the table reporting on what they were doing, or planning to do, so that everybody would know what was going on. One of the rules of these meetings, says McGowan, was "that you could ask somebody to clarify what they said, but you couldn't argue back and forth or we'd have been there through Tuesday. Now and then," McGowan adds, "one of these guys would try to put the monkey on my back by asking me to approve something. I'd tell 'em, 'You've got an interesting problem there.' "

Those Monday-morning meetings are long gone, however, since MCI's growth has forced McGowan to massively reorganize the company to align it with the seven regional Bell companies that are its main competitors. There are now seven MCIs, each one managed from the headquarters city of the Bell company it's battling. This allows MCI to put more entrepreneurial authority out in the field closer to the customer, so it can sell them more services. "This," says McGowan, "is the name of the game, since the more services our customers buy, the more important we become to them. This results in growth, which immediately shows up on our bottom line. And the growth is not arithmetical—it's geometrical."

But, cautions McGowan, when you decentralize, you run risks. The biggest risk of all, he says, "is that the lean, fast-acting management style that's made the company a winner will turn into a fat-assed bureaucracy where managers spend all their time writing procedures, forming committees, attending meetings, decorating their offices, building empires, and protecting their tushes instead of making things happen."

McGowan has developed a series of strategies for protecting MCI against the invasion of the paper-shufflers. One is to fill a lot of management jobs with outsiders. "I firmly believe in the Peter Principle," says McGowan, which states that executives tend to rise to their highest level of incompetence. McGowan also believes "outsiders bring in great ideas, and can say to us, 'Look, you dummies, we stopped doing it that way twenty years ago.'" McGowan also hires the best managers he can find, and then slaps "golden handcuffs" on them in the form of fat salaries, stock options, bonuses, and sleek company-paid cars. All of MCI's more than ten thousand employees can buy shares in the company at a discount after they've been there a year, giving them a piece of the action too.

MCI, however, is anything but paternalistic. "We are not a womb-to-tomb outfit," says McGowan. "We are not like big companies, although some of our new employees come to us and say, 'Let's do the things big companies do.' My answer to that is, 'Why should we copy the people we just beat?' I tell our people we're going to give them an environment, a challenge, opportunity, and, hopefully, rewards, but basically that's it. I don't believe MCI should have gym facilities, make an effort to know its employees' families, or even hold Christmas parties. We don't want to be all things to all people. I don't think you *can* be. You can't run a very good business if you get too involved with people's lives."

This philosophy of going outside the business for top-notch executives also applies to MCI's unceasing search for the best communications technology with which to bedevil its competitors. "I think we know how to buy and use technology," says McGowan, "but we don't know how to develop it. And considering the pace of technological change in this industry, that's probably a good thing. If you've got an inhouse technology supplier and he guesses wrong, you're in trouble, and sooner or later they all guess wrong. So we prefer to buy our technology from outside suppliers, and they line up downstairs, hundreds of 'em, saying, 'Here's what we're thinking of doing, what are you guys doing?' We tell them what we think, and they say, 'Will you take my piece of new equipment and test it for me?' And we say, 'Yeah.' They're certainly not going to talk this way to AT&T, because Western Electric's a competitor, and they're not going to talk that way to GTE, because Automatic Electric's a competitor. Occasionally we may have to develop a piece of technology ourselves because nobody else will do it for us. But when that happens we always turn around and license it to someone to manufacture for us, because we're in the service business."

One reason McGowan wants to grab the best technology around is so MCI can be the most efficient, hence the lowest-cost provider of services in the now hotly competitive telecommunications industry, where everybody's profit margins are under intense pressure. MCI's earnings plummeted in 1984 after four years of rip-roaring growth, as it encountered sharply rising costs resulting from the higher fees it had to pay to interconnect with local telephone companies around the country. While this squeeze on MCI's profits shows signs of abating, McGowan's hell-for-leather management style does not.

McGowan continues to invest more than $20 million a week installing new equipment and hooking up new customers. More new products are in the offing. And he's expanding into the fast-growing international phone business with all deliberate speed.

McGowan started MCI to grab business away from AT&T by giving telephone users cut-rate service. It was David going after Goliath, and how it will all come out depends on who ends up using its equipment and people most efficiently. McGowan constantly checks MCI's efficiency by measuring how much it must invest to get a dollar of revenue, and how much revenue each employee generates. "When we started out," says McGowan, "we had to spend $1.50 to get one dollar of revenue. Now we're down to seventy-five cents invested to get one dollar of revenue. We were also getting less than $80,000 in revenue per employee, and now it's more than $200,000. Our services are leveraging off one another, they are enhancing one another, and our communications network is providing the means for them all."

Less than an hour away from MCI by bus and subway is the ultramodern headquarters of BDM International, whose nondescript name, lack of products, use of a management system the authors of *In Search of Excellence* call a "logistical mess," and heavy dependence on military appropriations have not prevented it from increasing its sales by approximately 30 percent annually during the last fourteen years, from $5 million to $190 million, with profits keeping pace.

Star Wars Business

Most of BDM's sales and profits come from the application of its esoteric knowledge to designing, testing, and evaluating U.S. defense projects such as the following:

- The use of "Star Wars"-type, space-based, high-energy laser beams to destroy incoming Soviet missiles within several minutes after they are launched.
- Estimating the effects of extended dormancy on a military system's operational reliability.
- Developing new instrumentation to provide rapid and accurate patient diagnosis under battlefield conditions.

BDM's remaining work is done primarily for commercial customers, including:

- Design and construction of a solar power facility for Atlantic Richfield, which will be able to convert California sunshine into one million watts of electricity.
- Advice in optics, structures, and other scientific disciplines used in building NASA's soon-to-be-launched Space Telescope, which will allow scientists to see distant galaxies as they may have appeared at the formation of the universe, an estimated 15 billion years ago.
- A study for the U.S. Customs Service on the threat inherent in the illegal transfer of technology to potential adversaries.

BDM is derived from the surnames of Joseph Braddock, Bernard Dunn, and Daniel McDonald, who graduated from New York's Fordham University with Ph.D.'s in physics, scraped together $10,000 of mostly borrowed money, and in 1960 founded BDM in El Paso, Texas. The trio's concept was that the knowledge of America's scientists and engineers was growing so fast and changing so rapidly that it made more sense for even giant organizations like the Pentagon to contract for their services as needed, rather than build permanent staffs of high-priced experts in dozens of disciplines from fiber optics to queuing theory.

The three founders started the company because they wanted

to be independent and to pursue technical activities that interested them, as opposed to being executives and managing a business. So they quickly began searching for someone to run BDM on a day-to-day basis, and found this person in Earle Williams, an engineer from Auburn University who was working on an M.B.A. from the University of New Mexico. Williams had spent ten years working with the U.S. Army and the Sandia Corporation on nuclear projects, and with Standard Oil of Indiana as a refinery engineer, but "liked working with people more than with nuts and bolts." Williams joined BDM as a senior engineer in 1962 when it had seventeen employees, was made vice-president and general manager in 1968, and named president in 1972.

"One of the first things I asked the founders," says Williams, "was 'How big do you want to be?' They said, 'Why do you ask?' And I said, 'Well, each of you is working with two or three people on three or four jobs, and I'd like to know if you're satisfied with that.' Because that's what happens in some companies, the founders don't want to get so big they can't be personally involved in every job. Anyway, the founders looked at each other and one of them said, 'We'd like to be as big as RCA.' I said, 'Okay, I'll buy that, even though we're never going to be as big as RCA.' What I was looking for was whether they had any artificial boundaries, and it was clear they didn't.

"It took us ten years to reach $4 million in sales," says Williams, "which was a grim experience, even though it taught us a lot. The biggest thing we learned was that the old saying 'Build a better mousetrap and the world will beat a path to your door' is sheer unadulterated nonsense. If you build a better mousetrap and don't market it, what you'll end up with is a warehouse full of mousetraps and you'll be bankrupt. You've got to go out and convince people to buy, you've got to be responsive to client requirements, and it took us a long time to figure that out. You see, being good is not enough. You've also got to be where the market is, and since our market is national defense, we decided to move the company from El Paso to the Washington, D.C., area in 1970."

That decision marked the start of BDM's spectacular growth as the company moved ever closer to its biggest customer— the U.S. military establishment. In 1984, to illustrate how close it's gotten, the Secretary of Defense appointed BDM's president, Earle Williams, to the prestigious Naval Research Advisory Committee, and co-founder Braddock to a four-year term on the Defense Science Board. BDM's superb marketing has helped it to secure so much business that at any given moment it's working on upwards of five hundred contracts running from one month to more than five years, and worth anywhere from $1,000 to more than $40 million. The company wins 50 percent of the contracts it bids on, and as it grows it's able to go after bigger and bigger contracts (although profit margins tend to suffer, since bidding on this big-ticket business is hotly competitive).

BDM is also profiting from the increasing complexity of modern weapons systems such as the U.S. Air Force's F-18 fighter, which has twenty-one on-board microcomputers, all "talking" to each other at the same time, as well as from the speed-up in the introduction of new technology on which these systems are based. "Technology used to have a ten-year life cycle," says Stanley E. Harrison, BDM's executive vice-president and chief operating officer, "but the mean lifespan for much current technology is about twenty-four months, and then you have almost a whole new technology base to deal with and apply."

Risks are inherent in any business, and in BDM's the most constantly threatening is the abrupt cancellation of a major contract. During the Carter Administration, for example, BDM had fifty people working on the so-called "racetrack" basing system for MX missiles, which involved placing them on continually moving railroad cars in order to confuse the Soviets as to their exact location. "We got a call one Friday afternoon saying stop work—the racetrack is gone," says Williams, "and for fourteen days we did a lot of scurrying around to get those fifty people moved to new projects. But with over five hundred projects active at all times, the loss of any one is not a dramatic problem."

Matrix Management

People with cutting-edge scientific skills are BDM's only "product," and its ability to attract, hire, utilize, and retain these brainy employees has made it the nation's preeminent independent test-and-evaluation contractor. Investment experts at Merrill Lynch have called this ability "a kind of trade secret," but to Williams it's nothing more mysterious than "matrix management"—the system that *In Search of Excellence* brands a "logistical mess."

"The last chapter of *In Search of Excellence*," says Williams, "is called 'Simultaneous Loose-Tight Properties,' and it describes an aspect of excellent companies which is really the underlying matrix management culture we have here. But the authors have a hangup about matrix management, they knock it throughout the book, and all I can conclude is that they only found places where it failed. But it works for us."

BDM is so sold on matrix management that it devoted a special section of its 1983 annual report to enlightening stockholders as to how it works. It begins by noting that since the Pharaohs ruled Egypt, organizations have been managed by hierarchical systems resembling pyramids, with workers reporting up through blocks of management until they reach the big boss at the top. BDM rejected this system in favor of the matrix because the latter reduces paperwork to a minimum and allows its precious human resources to flow naturally to wherever they are needed within the company. It also encourages its people to select projects they'd like to work on, and to go out and try, with management's help (which includes a special course on how to write a proposal), to sell those projects to clients. BDM employees who do well in drumming up new business are amply rewarded. "Generally," says Williams, "what we try to do is figure out what the individual wants and then give it to him. If that's a promotion, or more money, or a move into management, or not a move into management we try to do that. We have five separate career ladders here, which means people can move up very far in the company without taking on any management responsibility and still get the pay, the perks, and the recognition which go with having done a good job.

"Some people only want to be technical gurus," says Williams. "Others want to run four or five small, $100,000 cutting-edge jobs in which you're exploring something. Still others are much more interested in taking one of those small contracts and building it into a very large multimillion-dollar, multi-year program employing hundreds of people. So if you think they're capable of doing that, you let them do it. You keep stroking them, patting them on the back, paying them, and so on. Matrix management allows us to get the most out of our creative people, which is essential for our growth and profitability. It's a way of freeing up the intellectual energy of our people, letting them realize their maximum potential, while at the same time avoiding a state of sheer anarchy within the company.

"Now there's a lot of conflict within the matrix system, as there's bound to be when you break out of the box of each employee having just one job and one boss. Suppose, for instance, that a guy's working on two projects, and the managers of both of them want him to attend a staff meeting at eight o'clock on Monday morning. The guy explodes. 'How can I be in two places at once? I can't work in this crazy place. I'm just going to go back and sit in my office and wait. I'm not going to either meeting.' Or saying—which is just as bad—'I like the manager of project A, so I'll go to his meeting and I won't go to B.' Both of those solutions are wrong. What the guy's got to say to both project managers is 'You fellows both want me at your eight o'clock meetings, but since that's impossible, I'm afraid you'll have to work it out and let me know where you want me to be.' It's not his responsibility to make that decision, because he doesn't have enough information. But it is his responsibility to point out that he's been placed in a conflict situation and let those who have the information work it out. A lot of people are uncomfortable in this type of environment, they lack flexibility, and we discourage them from coming to work at BDM."

Up until 1980, BDM financed its expansion through retained earnings and money borrowed from banks against accounts receivable from the government. The rapid growth in BDM's operations had made it increasingly dependent on large bank loans carrying high rates of interest, which are not recoverable under government contracts. So the company decided to raise operating capital by selling some of its stock to the public, which it felt would solve this problem along with several others that were equally pressing. Williams says BDM decided to go public for the following reasons:

"We wanted to be independent, to have our own capital to operate with, so no financial institution could ever again tell us, 'You can't bid on this job, because we won't finance it,' which happened to us one time.

"We found that the stock options we had been giving key employees lacked sufficient incentive value. Our people kept asking, 'What's BDM's stock worth? I can't dispose of it. I got kids going to college and I'm ready to convert this very valuable stock but there's no way to get the money. So this stock option I was very happy to get two years ago suddenly looks to me like it's not worth very much.'

"We knew that at some point we would have to liquefy the estates of the three founders, who were in their fifties.

"And, finally, we wanted a public market for our stock so we could use it to make acquisitions. We're actively looking for companies in the professional services business that are doing a quality job, but have a different client base than we do. In this business, marketing is the key to diversification. BDM has technology we believe other clients could use, and acquiring a company already serving that market might be the best way to go."

BDM became a publicly owned company on October 3, 1980, when it sold 400,000 shares of newly issued stock at $15.50 per share, netting it nearly $6 million (the three founders also sold 75,000 shares, thereby reducing their holdings to just over 40 percent of BDM's outstanding stock). In order to allow the founders to maintain control of BDM until their retirement, the company later effected an exchange offer establishing two classes of common stock. Class A stock is listed on the American Stock Exchange, receives at least a 15-percent higher cash dividend than Class B stock, is used for employee stock options and acquisitions, but can only elect 25 percent of BDM's board of directors. Class B stock is convertible into Class A stock on a one-for-one basis, does not trade publicly, and is owned almost entirely by the company's three founders and the CEO, Williams, who can elect 75 percent of the board, giving them control of the business until they step down.

That is not likely to happen for a while, as all four are obviously having the time of their lives. The business is growing nicely, the three founders continue to pursue their scientific inclinations as corporate vice-presidents free of management responsibilities (although they do serve on the board), and Williams is exuberant. "Every day people are coming in here with new and exciting ideas, so I'm looking forward to the future because I think it's going to be better than the past."

One reason is that BDM's dynamically growing sales still account for less than 0.1 percent of U.S. defense expenditures. Another is that Williams believes the amount of government contracting will probably increase, and that within the next two to three years the private-sector market for professional services is going to explode. "U.S. basic industry is going to discover what the government did a long time ago," says Williams, "namely that it doesn't make any sense to load your payroll with technical expertise you can contract for as needed and then tell to go away."

It's not surprising that BDM has reduced the strategy it plans to use to capture its fair share of all this business to something resembling a scientific formula—$Q^2 TC^2$, which stands for producing work of appropriate Quality and Quantity, on Time, with Controlled Costs. You'll notice how the first symbol in BDM's formula stands for Quality, which too many companies don't get around to emphasizing until rather late in the game, although recently this has started to change.

Quality College

Since World War II, the failure of American companies to manage quality has enabled the perfectionist Japanese to dethrone the United States as the world's leading producer of a great many products from automobiles to television sets. But now U.S. companies are fighting back:

- At Ford Motor Company, "Quality Is Job One."
- Xerox is offering vendors "life of the product" contracts in return for delivering "zero-defect" parts.
- Advanced Micro Devices has placed a sign outside its executive offices which reads "Quality is never having to say you're sorry."
- And the Tennant Company of Minneapolis, the world's largest maker of industrial sweepers and scrubbers, has a Zero Defects Day celebration during which employees and their supervisors co-sign a statement pledging to do their work

right the first time which has so far cut Tennant's manufacturing defects by 60 percent per machine.
- And the American Society for Quality Control, headquartered in Milwaukee, says its membership has shot up from
thirty-three thousand in 1980 to forty-five thousand in 1985.

Quality is hot, and companies that have never given it a
second thought are now spending thousands of dollars a day
to study the subject with leading U.S. quality-control experts
such as Philip Crosby, the originator of the "zero defects"
concept. Crosby has been in the quality-control business for
more than thirty years, starting out as a production-line in-
spector and rising to Corporate Vice-President of Quality for
ITT before founding his "Quality College" in Winter Park,
Florida. General Motors recently purchased a 10-percent interest in Crosby's little business in order to get closer to his
thinking, which includes insights such as these:

- Any company can reduce its incoming-defect level by 50
percent, simply by talking to its suppliers. One tip: make
sure your parts-testing equipment is identical to your suppliers'.
- More than 85 percent of all problems can be resolved at the
first level of supervision, and most of the remainder can be
resolved at the second level.

Crosby's credo can be summed up in six words: "Do it right
the first time." "But," he adds, "you must be able to tell your
people what 'it' is. What is 'it' you want them to do right the
first time? You have to set clear requirements, and then you
have to get a performance standard. That is where 'zero defects' comes in. The requirement is 'What do you want me to
do?' and the performance standard is 'How often do you want
me to do it?' 'I want you to come to work at eight o'clock every

day' is the performance standard, and the 'every day' is the 'zero defects.'

"The problem with quality," says Crosby, "is that people define it as beauty, truth, excellence—some kind of vague thing. You say, 'Bring me this back when it's excellent,' but how does anybody know what 'excellent' is? So we say you have to talk about quality as conformance to requirements. And most companies have requirements, it's just that they don't pay much attention to them. So you decide what you're going to do, you make it clear, you make sure everybody understands it, and that's what you do.

"What we're talking about here," says Crosby, "is really the price of nonconformance versus conformance. The price of nonconformance is the scrap, the rework, the warranty, all of those expenses you have to pay to repair things. In white-collar and administrative operations, the scrap goes out in wastebaskets, and in manufacturing it goes out in barrels. The price of conformance is what you have to pay in terms of education and quality assurance to get things to come out right the first time. It takes four or five percent of sales to do this prevention job. But by doing it you save about 20 percent of sales in manufacturing operations, and from 35 to 40 percent in administration and service operations."

Crosby will not enroll a company in his Quality College unless its chairman and president participate, and when they do, their attitude toward quality is completely transformed, he claims, going from what Crosby calls "uncertainty" to "wisdom." "At the 'uncertainty' level," says Crosby, "they have no comprehension that quality is a management tool. They figure you can't make anything right all the time anyway, and that if you have a good quality department you can keep it down to a minimum. The quality profession is looked upon as a necessary evil. Then they move up to 'awakening' when it begins to dawn on them that 'Gee, maybe there's something we ought to do to get quality a little better, but if it costs any money, or takes any time, I don't want to do it.' Next," says Crosby, "comes 'enlightenment' when management starts saying, 'We're just tired of all these problems, our customers are complaining, we get all this hassle all the time, who knows, maybe it is a management problem, maybe we can even do something about it.'

"It's at this point that management's whole attitude toward quality changes, and it's here that we can begin to help them. We tell management they caused the mess they're in, and what they can do to fix it. Suddenly, after they've got a quality education system working in their companies, their whole attitude shifts. They don't argue and fight about it anymore, since it's not subjective. If the requirement is to answer the telephone before the third ring, then you set up a system to get that done, and that's that.

"Once management gets through into 'enlightenment,' " says Crosby, "then they get pretty good at it and they go into 'wisdom'—and start making money. They start getting their investment in quality back, and realize that to keep it up, new people coming in must be trained, and old workers must be retrained. The chairman and president must go around and talk to people about the company's commitment to quality, and they must never again let themselves compromise on quality just to meet a short-term goal. But it gets to be fun, they really get involved. It's a whole new thing, like finding out you really don't need to have a toothache."

Crosby believes the commitment to quality goes on forever, but he also thinks it's important for companies to have short-term improvement programs—"something you do and then it's done." Crosby's favorite program is BAD ("Buck-a-Day"), which consists of asking everyone in the company to write down ideas for reducing the cost of their jobs by one dollar a day ($250 a year). When Crosby implemented the BAD program among his own staff of ninety employees, some four hundred ideas were submitted. Among them was the suggestion that if one page was eliminated from the response mailed out to inquiries from potential new clients, it would save fifty cents per letter. Employees who came up with winning ideas got a coffee mug imprinted with the words "I Had a BAD Idea." "But what the employees really got," says Crosby, "was participation. We all did it, and in these times it's up to all of us to do everything we can to keep the company strong."

Cash Cow(hide)

It would be difficult to find a business more unlike Bill McGowan's capital-intensive MCI Communications, or Earle Williams's knowledge-intensive BDM International, than Philip Kaltenbacher's cowhide-intensive Seton Company in Newark, New Jersey, which his immigrant grandfather founded back in 1906, eventually naming it after Mother Elizabeth Seton, America's first native-born saint. Seton's growth from a hide-tanner to a diversified American Stock Exchange company, whose sales have more than doubled from $44 million to over $100 million in the last five years, is the result of an adventuresome management expanding into a string of new businesses. "We've used leather as a 'cash cow' to nurture and finance fast-growing new businesses, almost all of which were developed internally," says Phil Kaltenbacher, 48, Seton's Yale-educated chairman and chief executive officer. "We pride ourselves on the fact," says Kaltenbacher, "that if any one of our eight hundred employees has a good idea, he can immediately get to me or our president, and if he can sell us, we'll give it a shot, provided it gives us an unfair advantage over the competition. By that I mean it's got to be in a business we already know something about. And it would help if we could make it using our existing machinery, or if it dovetailed with our existing technology, or if we could sell it through our existing sales force. We now have so many tentacles out there that the possibilities of attaching something to them keep getting greater and greater every day—tentacles on tentacles."

Seton started out in the side-leather business, in which hides are split down the middle during processing, making it easier to convert them into finished products such as shoes, belts, and handbags. In 1956 the company purchased a whole-hide tannery where entire skins are worked, thereby preserving the big patterns preferred for use in upholstering automobile seats and furniture.

It was also during the 1950s, says Kaltenbacher, that a young chemist "who had fire in his belly and was awful smart" joined Seton and was sent to work in its japannery in Wilmington, Delaware, where hides were given a high-gloss patent-leather finish by coating them with a linseed-oil compound and hanging them out in the sun to dry. The chemist's name was Paul Fertell—he is today the company's president—and it wasn't long before he developed a superior urethane finish for patent leather, which convinced the Kaltenbachers that Seton should go into the chemical business. The company started producing urethane finishes for leather, and then branched out into making impregnants, binders, and finishes for the textile business, and epoxy chemicals for surface coatings and adhesives. One of the companies that Seton supplied with urethanes was Norwood Industries, a textile-laminating firm in Malvern, Pennsylvania, which it later bought.

Then Seton got an inquiry from a major pharmaceutical company about a substance called collagen which is the protein in connective animal tissue and a by-product of the tanning business. It seems the company had developed a surgical suture made out of collagen, which dissolves in the body, and was casting around for something else to make from the stuff, when it hit upon the idea of using it as a replacement for hog gut in sausage casings. After an initial "goof" in meeting the company's needs, says Kaltenbacher, Seton got its act together and now provides the vast majority of the collagen used in making sausage casing. "We formed a new and very profitable business," says Kaltenbacher, "out of an old by-product."

Seton then turned its attention to its new urethane-coated-fabrics business, which was turning out to be riddled with problems. "It's a fashion business," says Kaltenbacher, "and it's dependent on whatever colors, shades, or patterns fashion designers decide are 'in' each year. It's tough, so we asked ourselves, 'What else could we make with this machinery?' The answer we came up with was that if we had some adhesive technology, we could use the machinery to make industrial products." Seton pursued this idea by hiring some adhesive chemists, acquiring some patents, and enhancing the technology, and before long it was turning out products that, among other things, could be used in fastening decorative side molding strips to automobiles.

Seton's next strategic insight was that it might have a future in the lucrative medical business if it could somehow fuse its know-how in collagen, laminating, and adhesives technology. "We fished around," says Kaltenbacher, "and ended up making some reasonably sophisticated wound-care dressing components for pharmaceutical companies." Seton was determined to find even more new uses for collagen, however, which Kaltenbacher says "is like a Shmoo—you can do the darnedest things with it." This decision sent Seton on an adventure out of a James Bond spy novel.

"We searched all the patents involving collagen," says Kaltenbacher, "and we discovered that we needed to contact a certain Ph.D. from behind the Iron Curtain whom we called 'Doctor X,' who had a patent for using collagen in treating burns. It turned out that Doctor X had defected to West Germany, where he was working for a pharmaceutical company. We convinced Doctor X that he'd be a lot safer in America, and ended up doing a joint venture with the West German pharmaceutical firm. The venture involved topical health-care products, from strong lightweight casts made out of plaster of paris to metalized bandages to sophisticated incise drapes for operations. We're also continuing to develop other proprietary wound-care products, such as moisture-vapor-permeable dressings, and components for transdermal patches which deliver drugs that diffuse into the bloodstream. So we fell into one more branch of the medical field. Another tentacle on a tentacle."

Kaltenbacher says that until recently, Seton's strategic planning consisted of a few of the company's top executives getting together and deciding "what projects we wanted to pursue, putting them in rank order, determining how much capital was needed, and then funding them. Today this is changing, because as we move deeper into the health-care field, we find we need longer lead times to obtain sophisticated equipment, put up fancy buildings with white rooms where the air is treated, and so forth. So we're changing. But our management is still entrepreneurial and innovative, and our lines of communication with our employees—who still provide us with most of our new ideas—remain short. This has been the secret of our growth in the past, and we see no reason to change," says Kaltenbacher, who will probably be the last member of his family to manage the Seton Company, when he retires sometime toward the end of the century.

By this time, winning entrepreneurs have succeeded in climbing the learning curve to profitability. They have mastered the art of building a moneymaking business, and are now free to savor the joys of running it until it's time to move on.

11

What Do You Do After You've Won?

"We are not managing this company for the next quarter. We are building it for the next generation."

—Samuel C. Johnson,
Chairman,
S.C. Johnson & Son, Inc. (started
by his great-grandfather in 1886)

One of the happiest winners in business today is Evander Preston, a tall man with a lion's mane of graying hair, who works in a white long-sleeved shirt, blue jeans, snakeskin boots, heavy gold and turquoise jewelry, and a white cockatoo perched on his left shoulder. Preston makes one-of-a-kind, handcrafted jewelry of platinum, gold, silver, diamonds, rubies, coral, ivory, and other precious materials, which he sells to connoisseurs from all over the world at very high prices.

Preston will never join the big winners (and their issue) named in *Forbes* magazine's list of "The 400 Richest People in America." Yet his small business has already given him a life-style of psychic and material opulence, one that should continue until he—like every other entrepreneur—decides to close the business down, pass it on to members of his family, or sell it to outside investors.

Evander Preston does everything with style. He has his by-appointment clients picked up in his white chauffeur-driven stretch Lincoln Continental equipped with cocktail bar, television, and movies for the ride from Tampa International Airport to his building on the block-long main street of Passe-a-Grille, Florida, a little town south of St. Petersburg near Mullet Key. Clients are admitted to Preston's establishment after pressing a lighted buzzer, being scrutinized from within, and then entering through massive double doors with foot-high golden handles cast in the shape of the letter *E*.

Once inside, Preston's clients find themselves standing in a quietly lit room with a sixteen-foot ceiling, suede-covered walls, parquet floor, white antique furniture, American Indian rugs, and a few artfully positioned glass cases containing treasures including a $2,000 turquoise and black lava rock necklace and a solid gold freight train devoid of price tag, whose Lilliputian cars are heaped high with gems.

Toward the back of the gallery, there's a raised semicircular display case with tall stainless-steel chairs on which clients can leisurely examine jewelry and gold miniatures, including copies of pieces that Preston and his European goldsmith, Owen Sweet, have done for others. There's a thimble-size golden pot with wooden handle and removable lid that a Cuisinart executive ordered in quantity for use as dinner-table salt containers, a gold bull fittingly commissioned by a top executive at Merrill Lynch, and a gold manatee made for folksinger Jimmy Buffett, who's launched a campaign to save these vanishing Florida sea cows from extinction.

Clients are then led past two slumbering Russian wolfhounds whose grandparents modeled for Wolfschmidt Vodka ads, down a narrow picture-lined hall, and into a kitchen dominated by a huge butcher-block dining table, which is surrounded by everything Preston and his thirty-one-year-old chef, Edward St. Clair (who also serves as chauffeur and chargé d'affaires), need to prepare a memorable lunch or dinner for his guests. The walls are lined with dozens of cookbooks (some by Preston's friend Annemarie Huste, who once cooked for Jackie Kennedy), a duck press from the Tour d'Argent restaurant in

Paris, a cappuccino coffeemaker, an Italian ice cream machine, a draft beer dispenser, four thousand bottles of vintage wine, and African masks. On the mirrored ceiling is a print by Picasso.

The meals that Preston serves for his clients usually go on for hours. They always begin with a golden sangria aperitif of disarming potency (one-fifth Chablis, ten ounces Triple Sec, ten ounces French brandy, stirred with ice and garnished with sliced oranges and lemon), proceed through exotic appetizers such as glazed ox tongue with quail eggs, move on to entrées from elk to octopus, are accompanied by a collection of wines (some bearing Preston's private label), and end with liqueurs, rainbow-colored Sobranie cigarettes, and Montecruz or better cigars.

Preston has handcrafted his life into a kind of jewel that enchants his clients. They quickly become friends who long to return to the delights of his establishment, and are pushing his sales toward $1 million a year.

Life is sweet for Evander Preston, and at forty-nine years of age, he's got ample time to enjoy it. But at some point he'll want to begin slowing down, which raises the question of his company's future. Since most companies are family affairs, most winning entrepreneurs eventually decide whether to turn the business over to relatives, sell all or part of it to others, or keep going until they drop (with a last will and testament spelling out what happens to the business after they're gone). Preston eventually plans to turn his company over to his daughter Heather, who currently manages the sales end of the business, and to his employees, who are practically members of his family.

"Eventually," says Dr. Leon A. Danco, founder of the Center for Family Business in Cleveland, Ohio, "the owner gets to where he really wants to keep what he has now—not grow. He doesn't want to work that hard, or risk what he has for what he doesn't need. It is generally only twenty-five to thirty years from the start of his dream to the start of his down cycle at approximately age fifty-five. Yet to an entrepreneur," adds Danco, "the business is his baby. Picking a successor is like letting your baby girl go off in the arms of a gorilla."

Kidnappers and Hit Men

Many founding fathers (and increasingly mothers) simply refuse to draw up a plan for succession, much to the consternation of all concerned. The frustrated son of a New York entrepreneur, for example, forced his father to leave the family firm at gunpoint. A wife, siding with her son in a succession battle, hired a professional hit man to kill her husband (he failed), and a father had his son kidnapped and held hostage until he agreed to leave the family business.

Passions can run high in a family business, and the trouble usually starts with the founder, according to Peter Davis, Director of the Wharton Applied Research Center in Philadelphia, which regularly conducts workshops for members of successful family-owned businesses. Davis believes that while the founders of such businesses are sensitive to their family's needs, in the worst case they can be headstrong, disdainful of others whom they view as incompetent (or competent but hostile), and paranoid about the intentions of just about everyone they meet. These traits, according to Davis, lead to the following behavior patterns, which make it extremely difficult for founders to turn over control of their beloved businesses to their offspring:

- Founders take criticism of their businesses as personal attacks. Family members soon learn to keep bad news to themselves, which isolates the founder from precious feedback streaming in from the outside world.
- Founders usually surround themselves with toadies who are

willing to be dominated. They, in turn, protect the founder from bad news in the hope of gaining his approval.

- The founder's spouse quickly learns to be totally supportive of his work and ambitions, thereby further increasing his isolation.
- The founder's first son grows up in a world where his father is all-powerful, and he soon learns that his survival depends on pleasing the Old Man.
- The second son grows up competing with the first son for the Old Man's favor, and along the way he learns survival skills and the art of forming family alliances to get what he wants.

All of this impedes the easy handing over of a family business from founder to offspring, which may help to explain why less than 30 percent of family enterprises survive into the second generation, and less than 15 percent survive into the third.

One founding father who thought he had devised a fail-safe strategy for passing the family business on to his children is Willie Stennis, a black man who nurtured Golden Bird of Culver City, California, into a $7.5-million chain of chicken-and-catfish restaurants. Stennis had spent nearly half his life building his twelve-unit fast-food empire and was ready to retire. So he decided to make things simple by giving each of his four sons three restaurants apiece.

Stennis's youngest son, Michael, a former University of Hawaii quarterback, did well with his three restaurants. But the other brothers lacked the entrepreneurial magic, and so the elder Stennis decided to take the restaurants back and reorganize the business. He and his sons agreed that Michael should be Golden Bird's chief executive officer, with the other three brothers serving as vice-presidents of accounting, the training of novice franchise store owners, and new store construction. Golden Bird is currently flying high, with its sights firmly set on becoming a national fast-food company. Michael still seeks advice from his semiretired dad, and dreams of the day when the Stennises will become the first black family to own a professional football team.

Planning, honest communication, and commitment are obviously vital to the survival of family businesses from one generation to the next. An early step in this direction, says Leon Danco, who's been counseling family businesses for more than a quarter of a century, is to have sons and daughters begin their careers outside the family business so they can make their mistakes unbeknownst to the Old Man. Danco feels that children should be brought into the family firm when they're in their thirties—and the Old Man's in his sixties—and have something concrete to offer the business. Danco also believes a family shouldn't hesitate to use advisers or an outside board of directors to help it get through the trauma of assuring the survival of the business beyond the life of its founder. "You must," says Danco, "perpetuate or liquidate."

A great many entrepreneurs, of course, do decide to sell out for a variety of reasons:

- They have no children, or believe their heirs are incapable of running the business.
- They have built the business to a size where it's being managed by high-priced professional executives so that their services are no longer needed. "They have gone from being everything to nothing—from doer to viewer," said Dr. William P. Murphy, Jr., shortly before he retired this year as chairman of Miami's $200-million medical technology Cordis Corporation which he founded in a garage in 1957.
- Or they may simply be worn out. "I'm so tired when I get home at night," says 62-year-old Murray Klein, one of the three partners who owns New York's famous Zabar's delicatessen and cookware stores, "that if I start reading a book for half an hour I fall asleep." Klein works from dawn to dusk, six days a week and several hours on Sunday, and

after 35 years on the job he's told his partners he wants to cash in his share of Zabar's business and real estate holdings thought to total some $30 million. "I'd like," says Klein, "to have a year—two years—to learn how to enjoy life before I die."

But whatever the reason, it's been estimated that roughly 20 percent of all businesses are up for sale each year. And there's some evidence to suggest that entrepreneurs are even less sophisticated about how to price their businesses than they are about how to price their products.

What's Your Business Worth?

A study done by Baylor University's Hankamer School of Business in Waco, Texas, for example, revealed that nearly 25 percent of the owners of 344 small firms in surrounding McLennan County "had no knowledge of how they would price their business for sale," and a majority of the remainder said they favored the meat-ax approach of basing the price solely on the value of their company's assets. There are innumerable ways to price your business, and since this could be the most important financial decision of your life, it pays to get professional help from your accountant, banker, or someone else who can suggest the pricing strategy that's best for you. The strategy for pricing a downtown furniture store differs markedly from one for a Silicon Valley manufacturer of computer chips, or a business whose major asset is a tax-loss carryforward.

Before taking out yellow-lined pad and pencil to begin calculating what you think your business is worth, it's a good idea to examine it from a potential buyer's point of view. Business broker Jerome S. Siebert, whose Siebert Associates is headquartered in Fairfield, Connecticut, has summed up his idea of what business buyers want to know in *The President,* a newsletter published by the Chief Executive Officers Division of the American Management Association. All buyers, said Mr. Siebert, are interested in the "Four P's"—people, product, profit, and potential:

1. *People*. How many employees do you have, and what is their background? What is the staying power of management? Is the firm union or non-union? What is management's relationship with the union or the workers?
2. *Product*. What is manufactured and sold by this company? What are its markets? What is the square footage of the plant, the condition of the manufacturing equipment, and the firm's expansion capabilities?
3. *Profit*. Have you prepared financial statements? (These sometimes need to be restructured.)
4. *Potential*. Where is the company now, and where is it going? What are the various reasons that account for this potential growth?

After you've looked at your business through the eyes of a potential buyer, there are three standard pricing strategies you should know about, with professional advisers alerting you to innumerable hybrid varieties, any one of which might be best for your business.

The most common way to price a business is simply to subtract its liabilities from its assets. In most cases this "book value" approach considerably underestimates the true value of the business, but its very kindergarten simplicity apparently recommends it to a great many entrepreneurs.

A better strategy is to adjust the worth of your assets to reflect market factors such as their replacement value or, on the downside, what they would bring under conditions of a forced sale.

The best of the standard strategies, however, is to price your business based on the profits it has generated in the past (possibly enhanced by future projections). Good businesses are moneymaking machines, and what determines their price more than anything else is the profits they can put into a buyer's pocket over the years. There's a back-of-the-envelope formula for arriving at this number, and it consists of (1) forecasting your company's annual future profits, (2) trimming this forecast to reflect business risks you see ahead, (3) estimating the life expectancy of your business, and (4) multiplying your company's anticipated yearly profits by the number of years you think it will remain in business. The obvious disadvantage of this approach is its subjectivity, and few buyers will accept your numbers without some rather stiff bargaining. A common way to handle this problem is for the buyer to accept your numbers, but put you on a "performance deal" so that if the business doesn't throw off the profits you say it will, the buyer pays less.

Once you've arrived at an asking price for your business, the next step is to find a potential buyer, assuming you don't have one in mind, or already lined up. Cash-rich companies, including giants such as Exxon and General Motors, are constantly investing in innovative small companies as shortcuts to fast-growing new markets in everything from food to telecommunications. The year 1984 was a record year for this kind of investment, according to Chicago merger consultants W.T. Grimm & Co. which totted up deals worth $122 billion involving 2,543 companies of which 1,351 were privately owned.

If your company has made a reputation for itself, you may get inquiries from potential buyers over the transom, or you might want to approach potential suitors on your own. You can also get help from professional matchmakers such as St. Louis investment bankers A.G. Edwards & Sons, which has put together a list of some 8,000 potential buyers, or New York's Bear, Stearns & Co., which is helping Zabar's three partners find a buyer for their business. There's a chance you can also get help from your accountant or banker who frequently knows of buyers on the lookout for attractive acquisitions.

While some buyers may be willing to let you take the money and run, others may insist you stay on until they've mastered your business. This is particularly true if the buyer is unfamiliar with what you do and needs you to teach him the ropes. It's equally true if you're eager to expand, lack the capital, and sell out to a buyer whose deep pockets can finance your dream. In this case you'll want to stay on to manage the growth for which the buyer will pay you bonus money.

Another way to "cash out" is to sell a chunk of your business to the investing public, with you yourself retaining control, as BDM International's three founders did in 1980. The experts who can help you do this are investment bankers who know how to raise billions of dollars from the investing public, but often have little empathy with entrepreneurs who want to cash in their chips.

One man who knows what it is to build a business, as well as raise money for entrepreneurs who want to sell theirs, is James D. Dunning, Jr., thirty-seven, who for five years was President of Straight Arrow Publishers, the parent of *Rolling Stone* magazine. Dunning left the publishing business in 1982 to join Wall Street's Thomson McKinnon Securities Inc. as Senior Vice-President in charge of its Corporate Finance Department, and then in February 1985, resigned to become Executive Vice-President of New York's Ziff Corporation, a large publishing and information company where his first job was to find lucrative places to invest $715 million Ziff received in 1984 when it sold off its consumer and business publications.

I talked with Dunning about the intricacies of "going public" shortly before he left Thomson McKinnon Securities which traces its ancestry back to an entrepreneur named Sandy

Thomson, who set up a one-man cash grain business in Indianapolis in 1885 that has since metamorphosed into an international financial services firm with assets of more than $2 billion.

The Trauma of Going Public

"The first thing we look for in an entrepreneur who wants to go public," says Dunning, "is whether or not we think he can survive the trauma of coming to Wall Street. Whether he can handle the vagaries of the marketplace, the economic environment, personalities here in the investment community from security analysts to institutional buyers, not to mention us investment bankers, who think we know everything there is to know about everything and whose instincts will decide whether the entrepreneur can sustain a successful public underwriting. And believe me, just as there are lots of successes, there are a lot who get through the process of putting a prospectus together which never gets out the door. So you've got a whole lot of entrepreneurs who get up to the altar, but can't get to the 'I do.'

"We've got a regular laundry list we go through when looking at a company which wants to go public:

1. "Size of company is absolutely key. You need a critical-mass business. We like to see a business with $10 million in sales, and $1 million of after-tax income at least for one year.
2. "We like to see at least three years of audited financial statements, assuming the company's been in business for that long.
3. "We look at the financial performance of the company to make sure it's trending correctly.
4. "We try to examine the relative position of the company and its products in its industry. Is it a leader, a 'me too,' what's its unique industry position?

5. "We look at the capability of management. If it's a one-man company, that's a weak underwriting. You may have a guiding light, someone who's the inspiration and the quarterback in the business, but you really need a team to survive in the public arena. You need a good strong financial officer, you need an operations person, so we look at both the entrepreneur and his team and how they interact. We also look at the way the entrepreneur presents himself to others. The way he speaks English, for example, because he needs to be a salesman, to be able to sell himself and his business to the investment community, which must sell his shares to the public.

6. "We look at the company's growth potential. It must show a historical growth trend, and it must have the potential for continuing or improving that trend.

7. "We look for technological obsolescence if it's a technical underwriting.

8. "We examine the company's competition, and we talk to its competition carefully.

9. "We look at profit margins and, beyond that, how the company really makes its money. A lot of entrepreneurs aren't willing to disclose this information, and even when they are, we've still got to conduct an exhaustive investigation for ourselves.

10. "We put a valuation on the business. Entrepreneurs come in and say, 'My business is worth $50 million, don't you agree?' We may, we may not, so there's this constant tug-of-war, trying to decide what the company's really worth. There are all kinds of ways to do this. It's neither a science nor an art; it's a blend of both. We look at everything from fair market value to present value. We also look at liquidation value, and at replacement value if an entrepreneur wants to sell part of his company. We do a spreadsheet in which we compare the company seeking an underwriting with similar companies that are already public. We compare

price/earnings ratios, debt-to-equity ratios, capital assets, sales levels, return on sales, prospects for growth in dividends, total stock outstanding before and after offering, all the business-school comparisons that provide something of a framework for valuation. The way a deal is marketed also affects the company's valuation. How well do the entrepreneur and his team come off in selling themselves and their wares to the investment community, which must ultimately convince the public to buy its stock? Numbers are critical to evaluating a company, but in the end it's the entrepreneur's spirit, drive, knowledge, and feel for the business that must come across if the deal's to get done. What investment bankers are trying to do, of course, is pick a value for the company which will stick when they price the deal, and which investors will validate later on.

"Doing all this can take three or four months. And since it's the entrepreneur who must take time away from his business to answer our questions and sell himself and his company to the investment community, his business can suffer. So the entrepreneur must be careful he doesn't neglect his business so it turns negative, changing its valuation and maybe even stopping the offering. The entrepreneur is also signing up for tremendous accounting, legal, printing, marketing, and other costs, and if the deal goes bust he could be forced to eat $450,000 worth of expenses, assuming it's an eight- or ten-million-dollar offering. Underwriters basically take very little risk, since an underwriting agreement is only signed the night before the deal is sold. This means the entrepreneur is at risk almost until the moment the underwriter gives him a check for the proceeds of the offering less its fee, which usually averages between 6 and 8 percent of the total.

11. "Finally, we look at how the entrepreneur plans to use the proceeds of the underwriting. There are three areas in which the funds basically get used:

- They go to retire company debt.
- They go to buy other companies, or to expand.
- They go to the owners of the business.

"There's plenty of money out there for investment," says Jim Dunning, "but generally speaking, there aren't enough good people to carry it off. People who know everything there is to know about their business, have the numbers to prove it, are long on staying power, and can impress those in the investment community thinking about taking them public. These are the people who will get to the promised land of a public offering and all the trappings of material success that go with it."

Once you've built a moneymaking business and have (1) cashed in part of your chips by selling stock to the public, (2) cashed in all of them by selling the business outright, or (3) simply taken the business to the point where it's throwing off substantial profits, you can begin reaping the rewards befitting a winner of the greatest game in town.

12

Life at the Top

"This is the most fun thing I've done in my life. It's a blast."

—Steven Jobs,
Co-founder and Chairman,
Apple Computer

Few entrepreneurs in history have grown so rich so fast as Xavier Roberts, creator of the Cabbage Patch Kids. While still in his twenties, Roberts went from being hard-up son of a Georgia handyman who eked out a living doing carpentry jobs to being a mini-tycoon mingling with the famous, from Hollywood movie star Bette Midler to former British Prime Minister Sir Harold Wilson. The country-road mobile home that Roberts lived in for years has been replaced by a ninety-room mansion he designed himself, with a gracefully spiraling slide connecting the master bedroom to the immense blue-water swimming pool directly below. And Roberts's old beat-up Volkswagen has been upgraded to an MG, a vintage silver Jaguar, two Mercedeses, and a Cadillac Seville limousine complete with sun roof, stereo console, wet bar, and chauffeur.

Xavier Roberts is a very big winner. And although there are many reasons for his success, the big one is that he stumbled upon an absolutely sensational concept—the first of the eight barriers that budding entrepreneurs must navigate before they can begin enjoying life at the top.

Roberts's great idea was to take the public's long-standing infatuation with lifelike dolls that can walk, talk, sing, flirt, creep, wet their pants, and even give birth, and drive it to the limit. Roberts's dolls are not dolls at all, but "Little People" born in a cabbage patch, with names and birth certificates, who must be adopted and cared for like any other homeless waifs.

Yet, as we've seen, it takes more than a sensational concept to build a great business, and Roberts hasn't missed a trick. He began with the support of four school friends who were each promised 5 percent of the business, which was quickly incorporated as Original Appalachian Artworks. He had his first Kids produced by local craftspeople, personally exhibited them at national crafts shows in eye-catching lifelike settings, then constantly enlarged his product line with new "editions" of his Kids ("Oriental," "American Indian," "Hispanic," and so on). He used his Visa card for free short-term financing, and bartered to get what today is his Babyland General Hospital.

Roberts was also canny enough to know what he didn't know, which was plenty. When prospective buyers at a crafts show stumped him with a question like "Will you take net ten or net thirty?" he'd reply, "I'll get back to you on that." He also recognized when he needed help, which led him to bring in an Atlanta advertising agency as the exclusive licensing agent for his Cabbage Patch Kids, which he had already copyrighted within an inch of their lives. When Roberts recognized the need to mass-market his Kids, he sought out a major toy company to manufacture and sell them, eventually settling on Coleco Industries, which agreed to pay him a royalty on every Kid they sold anywhere in the world.

But perhaps Roberts's greatest feat was to create a product capable of grabbing millions of dollars worth of free newspaper, magazine, and television publicity. Nancy Reagan gave Cabbage Patch Kids to two South Korean children visiting the White House, as cameras rolled. Bob Hope built a ten-minute skit around them on his Christmas Special. The "Real People" TV show sent a crew to Babyland General Hospital in Cleveland, Georgia, and when host Skip Stephenson mistakenly said on camera that the Kids "sold for one thousand dollars each," Roberts instantly produced a Grand Edition of his Little People, priced at—you guessed it—$1,000 each.

Young Xavier Roberts has already earned enough money from his Cabbage Patch Kids to live in Arabian nights splendor for the rest of his days. But like virtually all other successful entrepreneurs, what turns him on more than anything else is playing another round of the greatest game in town. "I enjoy creating," says Roberts, and the latest product of his teeming brain is a collection of "soft and cuddly Furskins bears" dressed in country clothes and workboots. The bears, says Roberts, came out of hibernation last spring in Moody Hollow just north of the cabbage patch where his Kids are born. And judging by the warm reception they got at the 1985 Toy Fair in New York City, Xavier Roberts has another winner on his hands.

Men and women determined to make it in a business of their own are coming out of the woodwork these days. The entrepreneurial imagination is glowing, and the resources available to anyone who wants to try to make it in a business of his own are unrivaled. "There is more entrepreneurship today, and it is somewhat different than before," says Alfred D. Chandler, Jr., Straus professor of business history at Harvard's Graduate School of Business Administration. "Society is quicker, more mobile, bigger, and more urban. This growth, combined with new technologies, has given the entrepreneur opportunities that simply weren't there prior to World War II."

The playing field for today's entrepreneur is literally the whole planet, with business concepts, capital, workers, customers, and more available everywhere. A Belgian cartoonist named Peyo creates the impish Smurfs, which are purchased by Wallace Berrie & Company of Van Nuys, California, and licensed to U.S. makers of everything from school notebooks to Saturday-morning kids' TV shows. Venture capital has been flooding into the United States from every corner of the globe, including the fabulously rich Tata family of India, which helped finance a Silicon Valley maker of super-mini computers called Elxsi, which recently merged with computer guru Gene Amdahl's Trilogy Ltd. Coleco Industries has workers in Hong Kong producing Xavier Roberts's Cabbage Kids. And after a long, Rip Van Winkle–like sleep, American entrepreneurs seem to be waking up to the business that awaits them overseas. When Ruth Cohen was struggling to keep her little family business alive after her husband's death, she suddenly realized "how foolish it is to keep all our eggs in one basket and not try to go international." Today, Cohen's Airpot Corporation of Norwalk, Connecticut, which makes a kind of precision shock absorber, gets slightly more than 25 percent of its business from foreign customers, most of whom live in Japan.

Technology, as Harvard's Professor Chandler points out, is also enlivening the entrepreneur's planetary playing field. Technological breakthroughs, from copier to computer, have long since transformed the way the game of business is played. Not only that, but it's given a few lucky players the means to build vast new businesses virtually overnight, adding a host of new names to *Forbes*'s list of "The 400 Richest People in America," for example, Ted Turner, Winnebago Industries' John Hanson, Hewlett-Packard's William Hewlett and David Packard, Teledyne's George Kozmetsky and Henry Singleton, ComputerLand's William Millard, Intel's Gordon Moore, Electronic Data Systems' H. Ross Perot, Federal Express's Fred Smith, Wang Laboratories' An Wang, and Apple Computer's Steve Jobs and early investor Armas "Mike" Markkula.

Electronics whiz Stephen Wozniak, who co-founded Apple Computer with Steve Jobs and designed the firm's first machine which they sold to hobbyists for $666.66, did not make the *Forbes* Richest People list because his fortune has been eroded by a divorce, high living (he underwrote two multi-million-dollar U.S. festival rock concerts), and other assaults on his pocketbook, leaving him with something less than $100 million. This was enough, however, to give Wozniak the where-withal to leave Apple Computer to launch CL9 Inc. (short for Cloud Nine), a home entertainment products company, with the help of two other brilliant engineers who designed the Apple IIc and Apple III computers. Steve Wozniak was ready to try his hand at a new business, only this time TV technology was his launch vehicle. "I've been really into computers for ten years," Wozniak told a reporter for *The New York Times,* "and that's a long time. I don't know many people who stay with the same thing that long."

The New Millionaires

Today's unprecedented entrepreneurial opportunities are cre-ating new self-made millionaires in every nook and cranny of the U.S.A. *Money* magazine estimates there are nearly 600,000 American millionaires, and that some 60,000 new members are joining this elite fraternity every year. "A remarkable num-ber of the new rich," says *Money,* "reached the magic seven-figure threshold not through inheritance but through their own efforts."

Entrepreneurs are also profiting from their slowly rising clout in state houses and the Congress, not to mention the growing appreciation of their importance among new-breed politicians, religious groups, and countries long committed to socialism.

In Washington, D.C., organizations such as the 500,000–member National Federation of Independent Business, Small Business United (a coalition of some fifteen small-business groups around the country), the U.S. Chamber of Commerce, and in Chicago the 2,000–member National Association of

Women Business Owners, are advancing the interests of the nation's entrepreneurs, as are entrepreneur-oriented politicians, of whom presidential aspirant Jack Kemp is the most visible. "Entrepreneurs are starting to get together," says Dr. Joseph R. Mancuso, president of New York's Center for Entrepreneurial Management. "They're going to become a force. They haven't done much on the political level yet, but it's coming. You can smell it."

The rising appreciation for the entrepreneur was evident in the 1984 report by the Lay Commission on Catholic Social Teaching and the U.S. Economy, called *Toward the Future: Catholic Social Thought and the U.S. Economy*. The commission, headed by former Secretary of the Treasury William E. Simon, noted that enterprise is "a virtue relatively neglected by theologians" and that the Church has put too little emphasis on "the practical insight of the entrepreneur." This report was front-page news the day after strongly pro-entrepreneur Ronald Reagan's landslide reelection as President of the United States until January 1989. And it followed the blockbuster announcement from the People's Republic of China that it intended to implement sweeping changes in its urban economy by introducing capitalist-style market forces, reducing government control, and encouraging entrepreneurship among the masses where, according to one slogan, "To get rich is glorious."

The organization men who run IBM, Consolidated Foods, and other giant U.S. corporations are finally waking up to the extraordinary productive power that can be unleashed by giving workers their heads. And, not surprisingly, entrepreneurs such as Gifford Pinchot III, who formerly worked as a blacksmith on a commune near Albany, New York, are setting up companies to meet this demand for what Pinchot calls "intrepreneurship," the encouraging of entrepreneurial behavior within the corporate structure.

Although the entrepreneurial environment is undeniably

better than it's been in decades, and although material resources, from money to advanced technology, are more readily available than ever, it still takes brains and hard work to make it in a business of your own.

On this front, nothing has changed since the days when a young Charles Revson would put Revlon lipstick on his lips and nail polish on his nails before he went to bed, and then get someone to wake him at 2:00 A.M., 4:00 A.M., and 6:00 A.M. to see how they were wearing.* Or when a young Calvin Klein personally pushed a rack of sample coats twenty-three blocks through New York streets from his shop to Bonwit Teller's, so they wouldn't be wrinkled when he showed them to Bonwit's president. Or when a little-known Lucille Ball defied tradition by using three movie cameras to record her "I Love Lucy" show before a live audience near her home in Hollywood, instead of doing it in a bare studio in New York with a lone TV camera, which was customary in the early days of television. This allowed Lucy to produce a movie-quality series that she later sold to CBS for $6 million.†

"What it comes down to is having a good idea and a willingness to work at it," says Ron Rice, a tall, handsome ex-lifeguard in his forties who founded and owns Tanning Research Laboratories of Honolulu and Daytona Beach, which makes Hawaiian Tropic suntan lotion, has just introduced a line of swimwear, and boasts worldwide sales of close to $100 million a year.

"I can remember times," says Rice, "when I didn't feel like I worked a day unless I had mixed the product, filled hundreds of bottles by hand, loaded the trucks, done the paperwork, turned off the lights, you name it. I had to kill myself physically and mentally or I didn't feel like I'd done a full day's work. My

*Andrew Tobias, *Fire and Ice* (Quill: New York, 1983), 63.
†Tony Velocci, "The Real Lucille Ball," *Nation's Business* (October 1981): 75–78.

buddies in the old days used to go out and party and drink while I was home working. I'd never go on dates. I just didn't have a social life at all. For years I'd just eat, sleep, and work. Now my buddies are all working, and I'm going out having a good time."

Bikinis and Burt Reynolds

The walls of Rice's office are covered with pictures of these good times, many of them connected with promotions for Hawaiian Tropic products. Sports-car races, celebrity ski tournaments and beauty pageants, palling around with Burt Reynolds, whose films he sponsors, and other Hollywood luminaries, and working with stunning photographic models in—and occasionally out of—eye-popping bikinis. Yet the only mementos Rice considers worthy of enshrining on a spotlit pedestal standing just outside his office are the original garbage can and broom handle he used to mix up the first batch of Hawaiian Tropic.

Though the rewards that will rain down upon you if you're a big winner are beyond counting, the one that entrepreneurs seem to treasure the most is having achieved what they set out to achieve. Nothing can match this personal triumph, including the cornucopia of honors and glittering treasures that are suddenly yours for the taking.

Honors are among the first to arrive as entrepreneurs gain recognition, usually well ahead of the time they convert their company holdings into cash. Ted Turner has yet to sell his controlling interest in Turner Broadcasting, although hall-of-fame awards, "man of the year" plaques, and honorary degrees (including one in "Entrepreneurial Science" from Central New England College of Technology) have been cascading into his office ever since he originated his "SuperStation" concept on December 16, 1976.

Foreign cars, palatial mansions, servants, yachts, and other *de rigueur* trappings of the good life are next to arrive—some exhibiting mind-boggling leaps of imagination. George Abhah, for instance, is a Wichita, Kansas, businessman whose interests range from oil to real estate and require him to spend at least forty hours a month in the air. Abhah is also an art collector, so it seemed sensible to spend $9 million on a private Gulfstream jet that can sleep three, has gold-plated bathroom fixtures, a steward who serves as chef and bartender, and $3 million worth of on-board sculpture by Rodin, Brancusi, Arp, Botero, Marini, Giacometti, and Henry Moore.*

It seemed no less sensible for Gilbert Kaplan to add a small, airy private dining room—complete with French master chef— to the headquarters of his financial publishing company overlooking St. Patrick's cathedral on New York's Fifth Avenue. Mr. Kaplan was concerned about his tendency to overeat in crowded Manhattan restaurants, and so he opted for quiet business lunches a few steps from his desk, featuring minimalist delicacies such as fried smelts in remoulade sauce, or boned quail with fresh red grapes. It is not surprising that imaginative entrepreneurs should bring a certain flair to whatever they do. Gil Kaplan, who recently sold his company to Capital Cities Communications for an estimated $72 million, has become something of a celebrity for conducting orchestras such as the American Symphony and the Japan Philharmonic in Gustav Mahler's flamboyant *Resurrection* Symphony.

Winning entrepreneurs are also financially able to make the grand gesture as H. Ross Perot, founder of Dallas's Electronic Data Systems, did in early 1985 when he responded to a request from the trustees of New York City's financially troubled Museum of the American Indian to build a proper home for the collection in Dallas, including a new facility spacious enough to re-create an entire Indian village, at an overall cost of some

---

*Leslie Bennetts, "Airborne Gallery with Berths for 3," *The New York Times* (July 26, 1984):17.

$70 million. Not long before that offer, Perot actually paid $1.5 million for a 687-year-old copy of Great Britain's Magna Carta, written in Latin on animal skins with vegetable dyes. The original of this extraordinary document, which the English barons forced King John to sign, limited the powers of the monarch and affirmed that the law must stand even above the king. Perot plans to put his Magna Carta on display in the rotunda of the National Archives in Washington, D.C., and then send it on a cross-country tour. Perot, of course, is a past master of the grand gesture. In 1979 he sent a SWAT team headed by former Army commando Arthur "Bull" Simons into Iran, to free two EDS executives held prisoner in Teheran's Gasre Prison. Simons succeeded, freeing the two EDS men along with 13,000 Iranian prisoners. Perot was less successful in December 1969, when he was refused permission to fly two jet transports into Hanoi loaded with twenty-eight tons of Christmas gifts for American servicemen held captive by the North Vietnamese. Perot believes, however, that his effort helped "embarrass" the Vietnamese into improving the treatment of United States prisoners.

The grand gesture reaches its most magnificent flowering in philanthropy, where winning entrepreneurs—and later their progeny—give away billions every year to underwrite the things they believe are important in life. A study of "The Most Generous Living Americans" recently published in *Town & Country* magazine lavishly illustrates entrepreneurial generosity.

TV Guide founder Walter Annenberg, for example, gave Israel $1 million in 1967 to help pay for the cost of the Six-Day War. Opera lover J. William Fisher, founder of the Fisher Control Company in Marshalltown, Iowa, has paid for fifteen Metropolitan Opera productions costing more than $2 million. Louisiana wildcatter C. B. "Doc" Pennington donated more than $125 million in Pennington Oil Company stock to Louisiana State University to build what he calls "the country's biggest and best nutrition and preventive-medicine center."

And investment banker and former alcoholic R. Brinkley Smithers pledged $10 million to establish the Smithers Alcoholism Center at New York's Roosevelt Hospital.

Entrepreneurs have always been intrigued by affairs of state, and the interest continues to the point where in America a winner's millions can smooth the way into just about anything the U.S. government has to offer. Rockefeller, Mellon, Du Pont, Harriman, Dillon, Heinz, and other old-money names have occupied almost every post save the presidency, while new-money names such as Watson (IBM), Packard (Hewlett-Packard), and Lautenberg (Automatic Data Processing) have also done well with one of their number reaching the Oval Office (John F. Kennedy, son of Wall Street speculator Joseph P. Kennedy, who himself once served as U.S. Ambassador to England).

It would be unforgivable to suggest that every entrepreneur turns into an art patron, or lusts after the Oval Office once his winnings surpass eight or nine figures. Many, like cat box filler king Ed Lowe, rejoice in more commonplace pursuits such as writing poems charmingly illustrated by his wife Darlene, living in an old barn they restored on their 2,300-acre spread near Cassopolis, Michigan, or buying 200 huge old pickle vats and using eighteen of them as "holes" in a golf course that's the site of Ed's annual Pickle Barrel Invitational Golf Classic where some 150 guests vie with each other to score a "pickle-in-one."

At one point, Ed Lowe figured there might be some folks in the good old U.S.A. who needed a hometown, so he bought Jones, Michigan, "the tavern, grocery store, bank, sawmill, I added a theatre, everything. Anybody who wanted to claim Jones as their hometown could register in the town hall," says Lowe, "but after a while we decided to close it down, so we sold it at auction for $500,000." During the auction, Lowe became intrigued with the auctioneer "who sold everything for cash, and every night took home buckets of my money. I had a hell of a time getting the money back," says Lowe, "so I thought this auction business is a good thing to be in." So he and his wife went to auction school, graduated, and started their own auction business. "We had a lot of fun in that," says Lowe, "until it started costing us too much money."

"I grew up tough during the Depression," says Lowe. "We didn't have any money and I remember burning corn cobs for heat, going without a warm jacket, and always having cold feet because I had to use paper to cover up the holes in my shoes. So today I collect jackets, shoes, and hats—I've got hundreds of 'em. It's nice to have money, and I've got competent people running my business—my 'Golden Cat'—so I probably won't run out. But my wealth wasn't sudden, it kind of crept up on me, which probably explains why Darlene and I still enjoy the simple pleasures of life like going into some of the grungiest taverns you've ever seen when we're on vacation and drinking beer and eating ham sandwiches, or telling each other when we go to bed at night what was the highlight of our day. It's usually seeing a little kid sitting on a stoop, or getting a nice smile from a waitress rather than some big deal. So we enjoy life. We have a good time."

To Stop Is to Die

So the rewards are there, awaiting the pleasure of winners whose long years of effort have finally paid off. But, as it happens, the one thing that winning entrepreneurs often want more than anything else is to keep playing the greatest game in town until they drop. Dr. Armand Hammer, now eighty-seven, who bought 10 percent of tiny Occidental Petroleum for $500,000 in 1957 and built it into a $15-billion-a-year business, runs the company with an iron hand, constantly travels the world, meeting with the likes of Soviet Premier Mikhail S. Gorbachev and Chinese leader Deng Xiaoping, and has no intention of stepping down until called home by his Maker.

"The day that I stop," he's been heard to say, "I won't be here."

In his book *Newspaperman,* Richard Meeker tells the story of a meeting between the two top officials of Syracuse University and the school's greatest living benefactor, eighty-four-year-old billionaire newspaper owner S. I. "Sam" Newhouse. The meeting took place in Sam and Mitzi Newhouse's sumptuous Park Avenue apartment, and it was soon evident to his guests that the man they had come to see was desperately ill (and a few weeks later would be dead). Newhouse paid no attention to his distinguished guests, being far more interested in the contents of a jar of candy directly in front of him. In an effort to ease the tension, Mitzi brought out some photos of a place she and Sam had looked at recently in Florida and were considering buying. Mitzi asked her guests what they thought of the place, and something in the question must have gotten through to Sam. "He sat bolt upright, and for a moment, as if distilled by the ravages of ill health and old age, his essence issued forth. 'Mitzi, don't,' he intoned, 'I'd rather buy another newspaper.' "

Index

Index

Index

Index

Index

245